Moonlight in the Desert of Left Behind

A Journey of Love,

Terminal Illness, and Hope

JAN BAUMGARTNER

ISBN-13: 978-0-9986320-0-1

Library of Congress Control Number: 2017901651
Jan Baumgartner,Sedgwick,MAINE

Cover and interior design by Joanne Shwed, Backspace Ink
(www.BackspaceInk.com)

Contact the author on Facebook Author's Page
(https://www.facebook.com/jbaumgartnerauthorpage/)

Cover photo of Billings Cove by Jan Baumgartner

For my Mother

And,

In memory of John R. Algeo,
my inspiration, whose courage, dignity, and
unconditional love gave my heart wings.

The only journey is the one within.
~ Rainer Maria Rilke

Table of Contents

Table of Contents

Acknowledgments

The year following our marriage we sold our home in San Francisco, ready for a new adventure living along the wild, rural coast of Maine. Less than four years later my husband, John, was diagnosed with the terminal illness amyotrophic lateral sclerosis, better known as ALS. It was an ominous day, to say the least; the last day of my 37th year and a precursor of what was yet to unfold. John was just 46. Without family or our oldest friends nearby, those new friends in Maine whom we had come to know and love offered their unconditional support, without which I am not sure I could have made it through the devastating years that followed.

There were many friends who stepped into the circle—too many to name, but you know who you are—and I'm forever grateful. But a few in particular I could not have survived without. Their friendship, love, dedication, and proverbial strong shoulders of support kept John and me afloat, and after John's death, they continued to be, and are still, my extended family. My gratitude is infinite to Parker and Carolyn Waite and to Dave Markle. The author, Doris Grumbach, our friend around the arc of our shared Billings Cove, offered not only friendship but became my mentor, often reading the progression of the story I was writing about my dying husband, and the heartbreak and complexities of both mind and body as his solo caregiver. Her encouragement was invaluable.

Africa too became a beacon of light. New friends, particularly in Kenya, gave my life a renewed hope, which held steady during the caregiving years, and my years of searching for meaning and useful purpose following John's passing. I will forever be thankful for those connections. These newfound friends, and the stunning beauty and grace of the African wild, nourished my passions and my spirit, and brought great joy back into my life. *Asante Sana.*

And lastly, to my late, great friend, Consuelo Mallory, without whom Africa may not have materialized and who gave me the greatest gift of all: experiencing with John a lifelong dream.

Introduction

I'll tell you how the Sun rose – a Ribbon at a time.

~ Emily Dickinson

When I initially sat down to write this, to try and pull everything together, it felt like a daunting task. How could I connect the dots, the years, the experiences both heartbreaking and joyful with the passage of time from when I first began the story, until today? How could it be neatly tied, seamlessly woven into some form of a succinct, chronological tale without causing the reader virtual whiplash?

All stories must have a beginning, a middle, and an end. As does this one. But the more I struggled with the neatly tied ribbon, the more I realized that my story, many of our stories, have nothing to do with neatness. Most of our stories, our lives, cannot be contained beneath a single, decisive heading but rather are all over the place, often untidy, scattered, threadbare, and fractured. Life is not always congruous. Perhaps that very incongruity is what makes it irresistibly exhilarating and devastatingly unpredictable.

I first began writing this story just two days after my husband's terminal diagnosis of ALS. There was no way to soften the blow of those words or the surreal images of a trapped body, paralyzed from the neck down, and the horrors yet to come for the dying and the one left behind. Soon enough, it would become our reality. Ultimately, the book was set aside as life became increasingly more complicated and frightening with the progression of his disease and my role as full-time caregiver. When I started to write again, it was in bits and pieces, scribbled-down thoughts and fears, dreams, nightmares, and at times stream-of-consciousness diatribe borne of John's suffering and impending death, and the loss of our future as I thought it to be. This is reflective throughout the book, and in order to stay true to my "voice" in what I was living day to day; the often fragmented complexity of emotions that inevitably became part of this singular journey.

Additionally and over the years, I kept detailed journals of my travels to Africa, with and without John. Those trips and the dream of returning were perhaps my strongest anchors, my hope. If Africa was my soul anchor, then nature, as a whole, was my intangible life raft; what kept me afloat, day to day, as John's life slipped away. The events unfolding around me—the sea and tides, bird migrations, the wild animals that frequented the yard, moonlight across snow-covered ground, bald eagles and fields of lupine—kept me centered and connected. And when I had time to dream, early morning or in the dark of night, the colors of Africa flooded my mind with vivid memories, the longing for the bush, the people, and the searing African sun opened my heart and mind to moments, although fleeting, of a hopeful future.

So, would this book be about one thing—John's illness and death—or about Africa and my hope for the future? For me, it couldn't be one or the other, for John's gift of love, and the hope of Africa, became the light that guided me through the darkest days of my life. And, in fact, in my mind they were inexplicably connected. I grew up dreaming of adventures in Africa, reading about its ancient landscapes and mysterious peoples, glued to television or books, anything that offered a glimpse into a culture and land that fed my spirit and inspired my imagination. Born from parents who had never traveled abroad, I became an adolescent armchair traveler, determined one day to venture beyond the familiar.

I made my first trip to Africa with John, when afterwards, and as destiny would have it, an article I had written about our trip that was published in *The New York Times* caught the attention of then Conservation Corporation Africa (now called &Beyond), which offered me and a guest an all-expenses-paid trip to any two of their luxury game lodges in Africa; my second during his illness; my third on the one-year anniversary of John's death; and my last trip just a year ago. It was John who shared my passion and my love of Africa. He understood my need for it, how it breathed new, healing life into me as his own life slowly began to fade. It was John who coaxed me along, who said with a final breath, "Go back to Africa; be happy again." It was a promise I kept.

Ultimately, with all my concern about life stories not being neat or ribbon-worthy, truth is, my story does have a common thread as it invariably returns to one place: home. A sense of home takes on many forms. I had the greatest gift of finding a home with John, not just the lovely home we made together, but more importantly the sense of belonging, a foundation of trust, one of comfort and peace in the loving embrace of our shared lives. My other home has been Africa. It is where my heart swells. It reduces me to tears of joy, sorrow, and hope as it is continually life affirming in all of its beauty, suffering, and resilience. Finally, I have found a home within myself, within my heart. As broken and splintered as it has been, miraculously it keeps rebuilding itself, reshaping in ways that allow me to feel all that needs to be felt in experiencing life to its fullest.

And, during the thick of it all, the coping and strides in coming to terms and moving forward as best I could, six months after John's death, his sister died following a brief battle with cancer. And, barely a year and a half after John's passing, my younger brother, 42, in a horrible car accident, was nearly killed and not expected to live. With a body badly broken, on life support, and in a drug-induced coma for almost 40 days, he barely survived. To add to the continued and overwhelming weight of premature loss that had become all too familiar, the last sibling and namesake in John's family, his younger brother, died of a massive heart attack in his sleep. All were barely in their 50s, and each of these losses came within a two-year period. What was left of my heart was wrung dry. But, as Woody Allen once said, "The heart is a resilient little muscle." Levity aside, it has not been an easy road, and to say there have not been very dark times, moments when I felt alone and forever lost in that proverbial *desert of left behind,* would be false. It was a long journey, which ultimately had to be traversed alone.

But the thread is still holding. It may be weaker, but as I have learned, time does offer healing, moments of unexpected wisdom, and clarity of vision and perspective, rising out of drowning hopes and nearly sunken hearts—from rigormortis to metamorphosis. As we are often told and desperately need to believe, "There has to be some reason for all of this, some meaning." Indeed, there must be some meaning, whether or not we ever fully understand what that may be, we must hold onto that slimmest ray of hope. After all, if not for love and dreams, however farfetched or seemingly insignificant, with what are we left?

Sargentville, Maine
October, 2005

PART I

Beginnings and an End

*Either death is a state of nothingness and utter
unconsciousness, or, as men say, there is a change
and migration of the soul from this world to another
… Now if death be of such a nature, I say that to die
is to gain; for eternity is then only a single night.*

~ Plato

CHAPTER 1

The Heaviness of Heart

Not till we are lost, in other words, not till we have lost the world, do we begin to find ourselves, and realize where we are and the infinite extent of our relations.

~ Henry David Thoreau

Sargentville, Maine – January, 1999

New Year's Day. A late-night squall has added an inch or so of new, dusty snow to the already existing 5 inches. Old animal tracks and footprints have been erased; fresh ones create a maze of life around our many birdfeeders. Cold seems a timid description of the day, frigid rather, a wind chill well below zero. Even the birds look cold, holding their wings tighter against their sides. With the thermostats at full throttle and the embers burning hot in the wood stove, the chill is palpable still. I feel a hollowness within, a cold close to the bone, an eerie emptiness. The winter scene of snow and ice and bending tree limbs, the black silhouette of a crow on a birch branch, only seem to intensify the feeling of overwhelming and wavering despair, making my life – our lives – seem somehow surreal.

Two days before a new year seems like an unfair time to give someone a diagnosis of terminal illness. And yet would October have been less of a blow? August maybe? Is there a good time to be told that your husband suffers from an incurable neurological disease, that the years you had planned together, the growing old together, is no longer part of the big picture? In the moments and first days following, your life changes dramatically, irreparably. Priorities change, rise, and fall; some disappear altogether. Your brain becomes thick with jumbled thought and emotion; you become frantic for time, not wanting to waste a single, precious moment, and yet so heavy of heart and limb you can barely move from room to room. Even breathing becomes a chore; each breath holds the weight of all fears and things unknown. All natural and to be expected, but realization doesn't always mean easier. Again, as in childhood, I am afraid of the dark.

We handled the news rather well. The hard part is in telling family and friends. We find ourselves trying to soften the blow for those we love, taking on an additional responsibility and weight of gently easing them into the abyss, offering tender, hopeful words, all the while fighting back our own demons. For most, denial becomes the common mode of defense mechanism, but this neither helps nor eases the outcome. Acceptance, no matter how hard to swallow, is the only way. Reality, like a fragile bone, must be acknowledged and tenderly treated. It does not mean defeat.

I found myself trying to stay strong while telling my mother that my husband suffers from ALS. She knows what this means, but the sheer horror of my words and the darkened images yet to come make most words meaningless. She offers a choked, "I'm so sorry, Jan," followed by quiet then muffled tears, a simple and honest response, no need here for additional eloquence. Those few graceful words and the sound of her silent tears were all I needed, speaking volumes, and the extent of comfort a mother could offer her daughter when separated by phone lines and an entire continent, those few thousand miles seeming like the ends of the Earth.

Those who know call and wish us a "Happy New Year!" with feigned happiness in their voices. Nervously, they offer this flicker of hope, knowing that our lives will never be the same. We accept their well meaning, although unsure of what Happy New Year means for us. Perhaps we put too much stock in that one day. Tonight, though tired from the ebb and flow of emotions that have been my day, I plan a New Year's dinner for John and me. A quiet meal, champagne and candlelight. I am not sure to what we will toast—each other I suppose, our undying love, the gift of our incredible relationship and all it has given us, and the tests it will endure. My initial thought is that champagne tonight seems frivolous, without meaning. But maybe a champagne toast and confirmation of our lives together are more deserving now than ever.

We enter marriage blindly, assuming cloudless days and smooth sailing toward old age. We say to one another "in sickness and in health" and "till death do us part," with naïve sincerity, not fully understanding the fragile cup that is life. Who doesn't want to grow old with their partner, their beloved? It never crosses our minds that the sickness and death part of our vows may come sooner rather than later. It's a heavy burden, sickness and dying, for anyone, perhaps even more so when that fate is handed to you while still in your 30s and 40s. Those are supposed to be the good times—the time for life plans, travel, family, and naturally good health. It is the time we hope for growth, both emotionally and spiritually, the shifting of priorities, the creeping in of wisdom, and the acceptance of the world around us.

Now, I look differently at other couples our age. They seem younger, carefree. I see hope and laughter, young children at their sides, that vibrancy of life and spirit that once seemed commonplace to me. But today I feel different from them. Older. Burdened down. I feel as though the weight of the world is shadowed across my face, as though my youth disappeared overnight, without a trace. Can they tell by looking at me? Do my eyes reveal the darkness lurking within? Can they sense that I do not stand quite as tall, that I don't fit in? Can they sense that I am different from them?

From our first days on Earth, we become increasingly afraid of death and dying. It's a topic rarely discussed with any ease or comfort. Americans do not seem to handle the topic well, much like aging. Yet, both are inevitable—facts of life that we treat with disdain or buried heads. If we don't acknowledge it, perhaps it will go away. How much healthier to accept terminal illness with grace and an open heart, as do so many cultures, than to shun or run frightened from uncomfortable diagnoses and those whose cards have been dealt. What options do we have? As I see it, we can go one of two ways: acceptance or denial. I fear denial must be much more painful because acceptance is like a dull ache—not unbearable but a palpable ache of one's spirit that just won't ease. But the human spirit is remarkable in its resiliency. I know with time that my ache will ease somewhat. While I have lost my "lightness of being," I am not defeated by our fate. Our lives have been too good, our love indelibly strong.

Today, at this moment, I feel no bitterness, no "why us?" But tomorrow is another day, and I don't pretend to know what it will bring. I also know, all too painfully, that now will be the easiest part of the rest of our lives. That the true tests of heart and human spirit are waiting for us, down that proverbial road. A road without a fork, without too many options; a path we must take. That realization presses a bit harder against the dull ache.

CHAPTER 2

Bright Beginning – Fade to Dark

You don't need a weatherman to know
which way the wind blows.

~ Bob Dylan

San Francisco, California

From the moment I first encountered John, I knew I would marry him. Oddly enough, I knew it before I saw his face. I had walked into his office (he and his business partner owned a communications, video, and film production company) to meet with him for a job interview. He was slumped over a computer keyboard; his long, wavy hair draping into his profile, wire-rimmed glasses resting on the bridge of his nose. I saw a partial profile, what I could see from behind the sun-streaked locks of hair, and knew. In that brief moment, and catching me completely off guard, I said to myself, "I'm going to marry this man." Destiny, I suppose. I certainly wasn't looking for a relationship of any kind but rather was enjoying time alone and with friends. But there he was—what I could see of him—the vision of an aging hippie, trying to figure out a new software program, while rock and roll music blasted through the speaker system. That day, we talked for hours. The interview itself lasted only minutes. We talked about our favorite writers, films, music, and travel, and our goals in life. That afternoon, the job became incidental. I started work the next day.

Over the course of the year I worked for his company, we became inseparable friends. We went to museums, met for dinner and films, rummaged through used book stores and vintage clothing shops, spent holidays with my family. We sped around San Francisco on his bright-red Moto Guzzi motorcycle, feeling the refreshing bite of the city air against our faces, my arms tightly encircling his waist, the warmth of his body pressing close to mine. But, for that year, ours was a strictly platonic relationship although I was falling deeply in love with him. The best evenings were spent at my apartment in the Marina District. We'd either meet on Chestnut Street for great Italian food at O'Sole Mio, or at my place where I would prepare a meal. Then we'd sprawl across the living room carpet with glasses of wine and my out-of-print Richard Brautigan books. After a year, I could no longer work for John. I was in love with him and, after that length of time, was unsure as to whether my feelings were reciprocated. So, I quit.

The evening I left, he showed up at my door. He had stopped first at the Chestnut Street Bar and Grill for a drink, more than likely two. Having gotten up the nerve, he walked to my apartment through the ubiquitous curtain of the damp and gray fog and knocked on the door. There was no mincing of words. "Okay," he said. "If we're going to have a relationship, we should talk about what we really want out of this." I remember smiling. He too had fallen in love with me but had promised himself he would not carry on an intimate relationship as long as we worked together. That night, no longer working for him, we held each other as lovers for the first time, and from that moment on we have never been apart.

Because of the incredible bond of friendship we formed from the start, our relationship has been the most trusting, true, and unshakable union either of us has ever known. We were together for five years before we married. It was the first for both of us, John just turning 42, I was 33.

At the ceremony at Stern Grove, beneath the massive limbs and shadows of ancient redwood trees, and with the rolling waves of the Pacific Ocean crashing in the distance, we were surrounded by our family and closest friends. Our good friend, Skip, an ex-Catholic priest, read from the vows we had chosen. In part,

> *When each partner loves so completely that he has forgotten to ask himself whether or not he is loved in return; when he only knows that he loves and is moving to its music – then, and then only, are two people able to dance perfectly in tune to the same rhythm.*
>
> ~ Anne Morrow Lindbergh, *Gift From The Sea*

And the line that has always defined our relationship,

> *Love does not consist in gazing at each other, but in looking outward together in the same direction.*
>
> ~ Saint Exupery

We are looking outward together, still.

It seems as though a good part of my life has been helping take care of others. John too had often been in the role of caregiver. His mother had become paralyzed from polio while still in her 30s and, in later years, developed cancer. John lived with her during her final years, looking after her needs, playing cook, to nursemaid, to companion. Later, when my grandmother died, the last of those who truly needed our help, we knew we could move on, start a new and carefree life in Maine; a life of fewer responsibilities, just us for a change. It would be an adventure, a time for new experiences, and something wildly different.

Just a year after our wedding, we packed up our lives, our lovely Victorian flat in the city, transported our two cats, and headed for the coast of Maine. We traded the city verve and bright lights of San Francisco for a life forever intertwined with nature along the wild and unforgiving sea. We fell in love with a rambling Victorian house, overlooking the sailing waters of Eggemoggin Reach and Deer Isle, smelling the sharp salt spray from the cove, watching eagles and osprey soar overhead. We had bought out of the city, ready for a quieter, slower life, one offering more meaning into what truly mattered to us. We looked upon our new life as one of firelight and books, walks along the shore collecting shells and sea stones, biblical sunsets, scarlet-colored blueberry barrens, and animal footprints in the snow. We did not know it would be cut short.

And here we are. Thousands of miles away from our closest friends and family, from all that was once familiar. Familiarity, especially now, when our world has seemingly ended before it barely began, when our lives have been forever altered, is where true comfort lies. But that comfort is not to be had. In a place that has not yet had the time and privilege to become home, it has suddenly become a frightening and unfamiliar universe. I look at a foreign landscape, cold and white, and try to comprehend what has happened, what it all means. But, for today, I cannot possibly know. Only time will answer the questions I never imagined I would be asking, not now. I suppose much of my life has been a rehearsal, a test run, and an ironic preparation for what I face next.

CHAPTER 3

The Abyss

Oh God! put back Thy universe and give me yesterday.

~ Henry Herman

*S*hit happens. I saw that bumper sticker the other day and couldn't help but smile. Humor has been the glue of our relationship. Somehow, even in the enveloping darkness, we have managed to smile and to laugh. We had made an appointment with a Bangor neurologist at the referral of our primary care physician, who was concerned over John's onset of muscle tremors. After a rudimentary 20-minute exam, we were told that John suffered from ALS, or Lou Gehrig's disease (named after the Yankee slugger). The doctor, before running essential tests and ruling out all possibilities before properly making a clinical diagnosis, told us in no uncertain terms that John had only a short time to live. We were shocked. We assumed the problem was due to a broken elbow that had never fully healed from an ice-skating mishap a couple of years before. Although numb from the words, John, attempting to keep his humor intact, looked the doctor squarely in the eyes and said, "Well, thank God it isn't a disease named after someone in the National League." This moment of levity was cut short, however, by the devastation of the doctor's words, and John, suddenly feeling unwell, fled from the room. It was the day before my 38th birthday—one I shall never forget.

Upon hearing of this premature diagnosis, our primary physician suggested we see a prominent and respected neurologist in Boston. We had a three-week wait. It was the longest three weeks of our lives. We were about to celebrate our fifth wedding anniversary and planning a trip to the Toronto International Film Festival. Suddenly, our world was spinning horribly out of control. Fading were dreams of sunsets and evening strolls along the beach, travels to foreign lands, growing old with one another. What we did not know then was that the next two and a half years would be a series of visits to Boston hospitals, myriad tests, collective head shaking and shrugged shoulders, few answers, and slowly progressing symptoms. Our lives would become a string of one doctor appointment after another, more blood here, another MRI there. But no one could give us an answer, a diagnosis. The not knowing became the most difficult part. It would have been far easier to have an answer, any answer, regardless of how devastating. Instead, we felt as though we were suspended in space, hanging on with both hands, not knowing what lay beneath us or what might happen should we fall.

So we lived with the uncertainty, not knowing if John was terminal, but clinging onto hopes of post-polio syndrome — one possible diagnosis because John, as a child, had suffered from polio and was temporarily paralyzed. However, John's symptoms appeared too extreme and, with hope fading, we were unsure of what another year would bring. Suddenly, any diagnosis sounded preferable to ALS, anything that was not fatal. But those slim rays of hope were to be extinguished once more, leaving us reeling from terminal to not terminal, and back into the abyss from where we began. It is an exhausting procedure, being told that you are going to die, then given the hope that you may survive, then having that taken away. We felt as if we needed to sleep for a good, solid week — just to catch up on lost dreams.

Like wading through sand, the months passed by. With a new doctor at Mass General in Boston—Dr. Robert Brown, one of the leading and most respected neurologists and ALS researchers in the country—John was tested for every disease imaginable before he felt confident enough to make a clinical diagnosis of ALS. When all else had failed us, the final test run was for adult Tay-Sachs, a horrible disease that usually affects young children of eastern European Jewish origin. When the doctor told him the test came back negative, John—not a child and mainly of Irish descent—shrugged his shoulders and replied, "I guess this means I have to cancel the bar mitzvah ..." We laughed, as did the doctor albeit nervously, knowing that the next words we would hear were more than likely, "You have ALS."

Amyotrophic lateral sclerosis: nearly as prevalent as multiple sclerosis, far more devastating, and yet many people have never heard of it. ALS is a progressive, terminal, neuromuscular disease that attacks nerve cells in the brain and spinal cord. Motor neurons, or nerve cells, begin to die, thus ceasing the brain's ability to start and control muscle movement. All voluntary muscles atrophy, or waste, including muscles used for swallowing, chewing, and breathing, leading to eventual and total paralysis. The mind remains unaffected.

Symptoms vary from patient to patient and can mimic various disorders. John's earliest symptoms included muscle twitches or fasciculations, pain, a gradual weakening of his right arm and hand. ALS is extremely difficult to diagnose.

There is no single test that can provide a definitive answer. It is a grueling, often frightening process of myriad blood and urine tests, electromyography procedures, nerve conduction tests, MRIs, lumbar procedures (spinal tap), and on and on. It's enough to rattle the nerves of Atlas. For us, it was a roller-coaster two and a half years of tests and the unknown before our doctor felt sure enough to make a diagnosis. It is a journey of ruling out all possibilities, regardless of how obscure, unlikely, or vague. Only then can a good neurologist offer such a bad choice of words.

I have worked in the field of AIDS, seeing firsthand the ugly grip of disease that took coworkers and good friends. I have taken care of and seen friends and family suffer from cancer and stroke. I saw my father's fight with alcohol and the horrendous battle lost when he had just turned 50. ALS ranks with the worst of them—terminal cancer, AIDS. Now my husband, still in his 40s, and I are in the fight of our lives.

CHAPTER 4

The First Lesson

But if in your thoughts you must measure time into seasons, let each season encircle all the other seasons, and let today embrace the past with remembrance and the future with longing.

~ Kahlil Gibran

I can see my grandmother's hands. Strong and wrinkled and tanned. Her entire life could be read across those hands. All of the hardship, the physical work, the sea of tears shed behind closed doors, secretly. She could set aside her pain though, like a book on a bedside table, from day to day, and continue with her chores, her duties—the routine that was her life. Part of her escape came from baking. Grandma Frieda's apple strudel. Somehow, from the mountains of flour, the peeled and chopped apples, the sprinkles of cinnamon and sugar, she could forget. I watched her hands many times, forming the dough. Kneading and kneading, her knuckles coarse and red. It was like watching an artist create; a potter working his clay, the pursuit of perfection.

Damp flour would crust around the simple, gold wedding band she had worn for some 60 years. Placed on a finger thinner then, less wrinkled, in a room on Ellis Island. She would work the dough for many minutes, across her dated, yellow Formica table, while I sat quietly across from her, studying her face, her hands. She knew I loved to watch her form the dough, and she would smile to see my amazed admiration. Never had I seen a dough so thin. After decades of strudel making, hers was perfection. A masterpiece every time.

She wanted me to know. To know the secret of the strudel. The secret she had learned as a young girl on a farm in Germany. The apples had to be sliced just so thin, not a heavy hand with the spices. Count the raisins; spread the sour cream with the lightness of a wand. But the true artistry came in the pastry making, and I would later find out it was not a lesson to be learned overnight.

"Now I will show you how the dough should look when it is done," she would smile, her German accent still thick after half a century in the States. A strong voice, a voice resonant of life. With her sturdy hands, she would gingerly lift the flat of rolled pastry, draped across her fingers, and hold it to the light. "It should be so thin," she would say, "that you could read a newspaper through it." I would laugh. But there it was, in all its glory: a pastry so thin, so glorious, and so ethereal that it seemed to command a moment of silent praise. Indeed, I could see the soft, yellow light glowing from behind her prized dough, and behind that still, her beaming face that only seemed to radiate to such an extent when her hands were buried in flour and sugar.

Her final words on pastry making were thus: "It should be so fine and thin that it looks fragile to the point of tearing, but it is not. It may look delicate, Jan, but it is very strong. You must be patient." That was the secret. And so I would find out, not just in pastry making. Many things in life appear fragile, delicate, yet there is strength beneath the surface, unseen.

Today, I wear her gold band. A bit worn and rough around the edges but a symbol of strength for me. It never leaves my finger and, when I'm feeling particularly vulnerable, when I need guidance, a moment of remembrance to carry me through, I look at the ring. It represents the strength and fortitude and love that was my grandmother. The circle of life. I learned many things from her. Just one being the perfection and life lesson of apple strudel.

CHAPTER 5

And the Beat Goes On

*The temple bell stops. But the sound
keeps coming out of the flowers.*

~ Matsuo Basho

The dichotomy of fragility and strength in life is always a wonder to me. Like the goldfinch perched precariously on a narrow branch, whipped about by forceful wind, its body somehow able to hold strong against the forces of nature. How can it not be swept unmercifully off the branch from a gust at 30 miles per hour? But it manages to hang tight, against all odds. Much like life and the resilience of the human spirit.

There are many things that drew me to John and many more that draw me still. Resilience is just one of them. He has not had a particularly easy life. And knowing of his past, I am all the more mystified at his contagious optimism and joyful outlook, something that has remained unchanged, even today. John's father died of a massive heart attack while playing tennis one Fourth of July. He was just 36 years old. John's mother was left widowed with three small children—from a months-old infant son, Clayton; to John, just three and a half; and her oldest, daughter Lis, barely six. As horrific as it was, that day only seemed to be a turning point for yet more family tragedy and a series of rocky paths that each child was fated to take.

When John was six or seven, he was afflicted with infantile paralysis from polio. He was paralyzed and bedridden for weeks but eventually regained all muscle strength and dexterity.

But the nightmare was not yet over. Not long afterward, his mother, still in her 30s, was stricken with the disease and became paraplegic for the rest of her life. On many levels, it was unfathomable what this woman endured. To lose her husband seemed unfair enough, but there were also three fatherless children to contend with. And just when she might have begun to come to terms with the loss of her husband and her family's future, polio took her mobility as well, any last flicker of normalcy or independence she may have claimed, and all before she had turned 40.

The years that followed were difficult for all concerned. Following her paralysis, John's mother was placed in a rehab hospital for nearly a year. The children were moved to another home that would accommodate her wheelchair and handicap upon her return, and were cared for by a distant relative. When his mother returned home, she seemed to shut down, as John put it, seemingly unable to give or show love toward her children in the very way small children so desperately need and crave it. They had been parentless for that year; now, with her home, they felt as though a stranger had entered their lives. But who could blame her or pass judgment? Her days of lightness, of happiness and good health, and of a promising future were stripped from her, leaving her alone in a metal chair to watch three, affection-starved children find a helpless and sorry joy in taunting her, dismissing her authority. Eventually, her daughter eloped at 17, finding love where she could, and her sons, John and Clay, were sent to private institutions or boy's homes.

As time passed, John's mother moved to Marin County outside of San Francisco, where John had earlier moved. Upon her diagnosis of cancer and until her death, John lived alongside his mother, filling his days in the role of caregiver; doing for his mother many of the very things she had stopped doing for him as a child. In some respects, he felt as though he had given up many of his prime years, from his late 20s until early 30s, putting on hold much of his life to act as a primary caregiver. But, with the passage of time, the wisdom and compassion that comes with experience and proverbial hindsight enveloped him. He held no grudges and, on occasion, looks back on those days with great affection.

So many people cast unfair blame on parents, on life experiences, and for all that is wrong or unpleasant in their adult lives. Some bounce back; some never recover. I've always believed that people must get on with their lives; move forward in whatever capacity they can; make peace with the past or, at the very least, learn from the hardships and nightmares that plagued them. That is the best we can do with the one life we have. John has done this better than anyone I have ever known. He has never seen himself as a victim, only of circumstance. He has made the most of his life, filled each day with a richness of happiness and laughter, and has never been bitter over the hand that he was dealt while still a young child. Perhaps the extraordinary conditions under which he lived and survived better prepared him to cope with life, and the final blow dealt while in the prime of his years.

However odd or seemingly hard to comprehend, these events have given John not only a depth of wisdom but a unique lightness of spirit. Something I saw early on, deep within his pale blue eyes. From the lack of a father, and all those singular experiences from which a father and son form lifelong bonds, to the disappearance of a mother's unconditional love and attention, John has overcompensated in the areas of loving and giving, and of taking care. He does these things better than most—with devotion, grace, patience, and good humor. I have been blessed to be on the receiving end of his infinite generosity. That is only part of John's many gifts.

Throughout John's illness, I have yet to see him waver from his positive attitude, his beliefs. He doesn't dwell on the difficulties of what the future holds, but rather he deals with each new day and what it has to offer. When you ruminate too much about what's down that road, you lose sight of the present. He does not complain. How is that, I wonder? I would. He watches his body change, and I see the concern on his face. His right arm has begun to atrophy, his hand losing muscle mass and much of its dexterity. It is changing shape, losing shape, looking different. He is learning to use his left hand and is getting quite adept at it. It seems to have come naturally to him. Can't grip the cup with your right, use your left. It was such a subtle change, I'm not sure I saw it happen. One night at dinner, he was eating with his left hand. There was no fanfare, just the quiet reassurance for both of us that he was accepting each new challenge without self-pity and doing what must be done to live as normal a life as possible.

Sometimes, when he is not aware of it, I look at him. He appears so normal, so healthy. If you didn't know better, you would never imagine such a disease was at play within. I watch him reading, eating, looking through binoculars at an eagle circling the cove. Nothing appears different. But everything has changed. I don't know how long he will look as though nothing plagues him. When will the changes not be so subtle? It's hard to imagine that he's not well, his disease terminal. At times, I cannot believe it, seeing the vibrancy in his smiling face, hearing his infectious laughter. This is dying? As I sit here, am I watching him die slowly? Does each moment take a bit more away, unbeknownst to us? What will happen to all of this life, all of this love? Where on Earth will it all go?

At night, in the dark, is when I become the most frightened. Darkness always seems to intensify fear, making the unknown all the more threatening. As he slips off to sleep, I lie next to him, feeling the warmth of his body. It's then that I am aware of the constant fasciculations (twitching) that ripple and wave across his body. While I know these tremors are always present, it's at bedtime, when my body is against his, that I am reminded things are not right. I always pray they will miraculously stop. "Stop!" I scream, silently. Maybe if I concentrate hard enough, I can ease away his pain, the fasciculations. But it never works. I would gladly transfer the shaking and aching of his body onto mine, if only to give him a break from the burden that has become commonplace for him.

From the darkened corners of my thoughts and fears, I tremble at what frightens me most. These are my own private horrors. Things I cannot, would not, share with John. Not yet. It's too soon, the wound too raw. When I think of these things, and they cannot be thought of too often for fear of crippling overwhelm, I feel a heaviness on my chest, a palpable weight. It's hard to breathe. Tears well up and trickle, quietly, down the sides of my face and onto the pillow. That darkest corner, the most forbidding corner in my thoughts, holds the nightmare of lost voices. Lost laughter. At some point, his voice will cease. What will I do when I can no longer hear him speak? He is a talker, a joker, and a wonderful storyteller. He loves to talk, and I love to listen to him. His voice has given me the gift of many, many jokes and stories, kept promises and dreams. It has been a warm blanket, a cradle when I have been ill or sad, tender words as smooth as silk, and comforting. Before I first met him, I heard his voice. I remember thinking how silken, how calm it was. His is an honest voice. I cannot bear the thought of never hearing him speak again, never hearing his laugh, his "I love you's," his emotional response at the incredible sight of an autumnal sunset or the arrival of a flock of spring migrants.

CHAPTER 6

Scenes of Winter

On wings of song, my dearest, I will carry you off.

~ Heinrich Heine

This morning, from the dining-room window, I watched John shovel a pathway to the lower birdfeeder. His right hand and arm hung abnormally, and I was well aware of the marked loss of strength and dexterity. Determined to see that the birds were taken care of, he gripped the shovel as best he could. The snow was nearly a foot deep but, fortunately, light and powdery. The pathway was necessary in order to fill the tube feeder and scatter seed across the snow. As temperatures have been well below zero and wind chills nearing 30 below, it's imperative to broadcast mixed seed daily as the birds have come to rely upon us. Although it was bitterly cold, John seemed to be enjoying himself. Once the path was cleared, he stopped and looked skyward into the depths of sparkling blue and scattered clouds, toward the cove, steaming with sea smoke, and into the dense tree line beyond. The meadow was blanketed with glistening snow crystals rolling down to the sea. It was a gorgeous day. So many people look but see nothing—John was not only seeing but absorbing every gift of nature before him.

I continued to watch him from behind the old, rippled-glass windows, all the while aware that I was smiling. What more can one wish for than true contentment? It was his and, in return, mine. He began his high-pitched chickadee call and, before he could repeat it, the air was filled with birds. There must have been at least a dozen, one at a time, flying in, dipping and darting in their acrobatic way, chattering noisily at the promise of feed.

The chickadees know and trust him; they know his voice. I laughed as I watched them zip by his head, barely missing, back and forth to the feeder just inches away. As he slowly crouched to the ground, they landed near his feet to take a seed from the snow. When he came in, hunched over and worn, his hands were stiff, his face cold and red, but there was a smile from ear to ear.

I sometimes look for answers at the cove. Most of my walks and journeys along the stretch of our cove have been alone, with my solitude. It's usually there that my mind wanders freely, and I look for answers that cannot always be found from behind my windows. Walking slowly along the beach, my feet sinking into the soft sand and discarded mussel shells, I look out to the green and calm waters and watch a family of ducks or a lone loon, moving effortlessly across the surface. What is it about the sea that brings all emotions to the forefront, all questions raging forth? I have a love affair with the ocean. I was raised along the Pacific and now look for, but don't always find, my answers from the cold Atlantic. Why do some of us go through life sailing across calm waters with hardly a wake or disturbance along the way? And others must contend with rough seas and fierce winds that only, on occasion, relax and offer safe passage? What a bumpy ride my life has been. And yet, in truth, however hard to accept, I wouldn't trade even the darkest moments for only sunshine. We learn from those darkest times when we are forced to look within ourselves for comfort and guidance and, ultimately, peace. If we must never go beyond our own surface, what depths or understanding can we hope to find in others? Fishing from those darkened corners, we can hope to find a commonality with others. We find compassion and insight, empathy and wisdom. We find answers that hopefully will guide us through the next turbulent wave, a strength to hold on to when the last of the waves rushes over us.

The cove, now, is locked in ice. Great, frozen blocks and shards dominate the beach and stretch into the water. They boom, reverberate, moan, and hiss as they shift from the incoming tides. From this cold and frozen world, I ask my biggest question yet, the most profound, one to which there is no answer: "Why John?" I know the question should be, "Why not John?" for disease can find a home in anyone's body. I am not a religious person but think in terms of spirituality. But there are moments when I find myself asking why God would take one of his kindest, most generous of creations. I have never known anyone as giving as John. He has been and continues to be a source of daily inspiration to me and to others as well. What will the Earth gain by his loss, his absence? I can think of nothing. What lesson is there to be learned in his suffering? Or the suffering of a child — or anyone, for that matter? I don't look for answers written in books and taken as gospel. I look into the infinite waters of the cove and from the depths of my being, and hope that somehow an answer, or at least comfort, will rise from the cold, salt spray or radiate from my fingertips.

I was having tea with my friend, Doris, who lives on the other side of the cove. We were discussing John's illness, life plans, and travel. I mentioned that I had not really broken down and cried over John's fate, our fate. One of those good, long, hard cries, a monumental release of the scramble of emotions that has welled up inside. I said that a friend of mine from San Francisco was concerned over this, suggested that I allow myself this release, and that perhaps I had been trying too hard to be overly brave. I thought she had a point. I had only been able to shed a few tears here and there, tiny releases of pent-up fears and emotions, but the tears were always short lived. "Well," said my friend, "maybe all the small cries have added up to one big one." This made me laugh, and I agreed that maybe this was true. For some reason, her words — her "realization" that my small pockets of tears may have, in actuality, runneth my cup over — was of comfort to me. That night, as I lay in bed, I again thought of her words and smiled.

Yesterday, following another night of hard freeze, John decided the local pond would be ideal for ice skating. He knows of my concern and gently eases my mind with assurances that he will be careful, pad his elbows and knees. I cannot tell him not to go; that, if he falls and injures himself, it will only make matters worse. He knows these things. I will not put up blockades or obstacles nor refuse to let him revel in life's small pleasures, especially now. Now is all we have. We are painfully aware that each day takes a little more away. It's difficult for him to lace up and tighten the strings on his skates. His fingers don't work properly, and they easily fatigue. His right foot is beginning to roll to the side, outward, causing his balance and gait to be off. He is acutely aware that this makes skating even more precarious. A serious fall on the ice could possibly speed up the progression of his ALS symptoms.

In less than an hour, he returned home. He was flushed and out of breath. "How was it?" I ask. "Good," he says, then pauses. He fell twice. He assures me that he buffered his falls by bending his knees and rolling onto his shoulder as he hit the ice. He is agitated and wants to talk. He needs to tell me something. "I can't give up skating or anything else I love to do," he begins, his voice cracking. "Otherwise, I'm giving in to this thing, letting it run my life. I won't do it." I nod and tell him I understand. "I'll have to make adjustments, know and respect my limitations, not just in skating, but in everything I do." His voice is passionate and thick with emotion. These challenges are becoming part of his daily life now. He is determined to buck heads with this disease, continue to live his life as he has always done—to its fullest. He can make adjustments here and there, compensations. And I'll do everything in my power to clear each path.

Blue jays belong to the family of birds known as Corvidae, often referred to as corvids. The family includes crows and ravens, considered to be among the most intelligent of bird species. Blue jays are no exception and, while a bit raucous and aggressive at times, we love their range of calls and mimicking of other birds, their lovely blue coats, and their gentleness and concern for their family members. They are the first to sound the alarm when a goshawk or sharp-shinned hawk is in the yard, and they have saved many songbirds from the talons of predators.

This morning, as I prepared to step into the snow and ice for the morning ritual of scattering seed, I heard a commotion outside, the screaming of birds. I stepped onto the deck, and the frigid air was pierced with high-pitched shrieks. They were blue jays, crying, but not their usual cry of alarm, of a predator close by. This was a far more desperate sound and seemed to be coming from somewhere within the stand of pine trees near our deck. I quietly made my way down, through the trees and bramble, the snow pack buffeting my footsteps. Silently, I moved toward the collective cries. Not far into the growth was the cause of the commotion. Lying on a fresh bed of snow and scattered pine needles was the lifeless body of a blue jay. What remained were the perfect and lovely head and shoulders; the rest had been eaten away. Wedged in its shiny, black beak were sunflower seeds, remnants of yesterday's broadcast. What astonished me most, however, was the happening going on around me. Surrounding the dead jay were five others — alive and perched in low branches and scrub, the family of blue jays encircling the body of their fallen relative. They formed what appeared to be a tight and deliberate circle around the dead jay, just a few feet off the ground, each calling in alarm, a personal cry and response to the death of a family member.

I stood outside the circle of mourning and watched them for some time. They saw me standing there, a witness to their tragedy, but didn't fly off in alarm. Instead, they stayed close to the body, seemingly in a protective manner, and cried at the loss. The scene was profound and deeply touched me.

When people say that animals have no feelings, no sense of emotion, I stand witness to this scene of despair, of sadness, of familial ties, and know otherwise. I do not believe that had this family of jays come across the dead body of a sparrow, a squirrel, they would have engaged in such a mournful and alarmist response. What I have seen this day is plain and simple: the ritual and mourning of a family over the death of one of their own.

Last night, I watched John strumming his cherished guitar. The instrument offers him great joy, comfort, and a momentary escape from a world rapidly closing in. I can see it in his face. That too for his beloved motorcycle. These two objects have always represented passion and freedom for John. From the earliest days of our relationship, I saw the wonderful connection and peace that John found in music. And when riding his motorcycle through the streets of San Francisco, the Marin headlands, or along Maine's tranquil country roads, it was exhilaration and wild abandon that fed his soul. It's heartbreaking now when I watch his fingers strumming. They don't maneuver with ease. He played beautifully, once. No longer effortless, it's now a struggle. The loss of dexterity, the obvious atrophying of his hand, all makes difficult the ability to strum, to make music. And yet he continues to play. His brother altered the shape of a few guitar picks to make it easier for John. It has helped. There is always a look on his face, within his eyes, when he plays his guitar, not only of contentment but of something deeper. It is a place I cannot go.

With bittersweet fondness, I recall the countless times I sat on the back of John's motorcycle, my arms closed tightly around his thin waist, thrilled at the speed and motion, the wind through my hair. We have enjoyed many rides together. But lately, he has spoken of selling his bike. This coming summer, he says, might be a good time to put it up for sale. He knows of the danger in not being able to get a good grip on the handlebars, not having the strength to manage the weight of the bike. I cannot bear the thought of him giving it up. His motorcycle and his guitar are integral parts of him — they nourish his soul, set his spirit free.

His guitar and his motorcycle — two objects, but true gifts to his heart. He will continue to play his guitar no matter what it takes. Sweet sounds still drift from his strings. He still escapes to that beautiful place, that solitary world where I cannot venture. It's his alone and mine to savor from the outside. His days of riding are coming to an end. He will know when the time is right. He will know when the freedom and wings he found riding on the back of the wind must be found somewhere else. So many losses and only the beginning. But I know John. And I know he will find it in another place. He is especially good at that.

The other day, February 13th, John and I watched in awe as two adult bald eagles, wingtips nearly touching, soared side by side along the cove. Their beautiful acrobatics continued for some time, followed by the pair alighting in a dead pine tree on the opposite side of the shore. They sat on the same branch, only a few feet separating their bodies.

Excitedly, I pulled one of my bird-behavior books from the shelf and searched for answers to this extraordinary display. It seems as though pairing bald eagles will soar together near the nesting site, occasionally chasing one another, diving, and, as we had witnessed, locking talons while doing a tumble-down, free-for-all in the sky. It's a remarkable thing to see, bald eagles locking talons. Their huge, strong bodies, roller-coasting through the air, tumbling toward the ocean's surface only to quickly unlock talons and soar skyward. During the course of the day, I would grab my binoculars to see if the eagles were still on the mating branch. For over three hours they remained there, looking stoic and proud, holding court over all life forms and actions taking place along the frozen stretch of cove. It was a lovely sight.

The following morning, February 14th, John handed me a Valentine's card. The painting on the front by a local Maine artist was of a beautiful bald eagle. Inside, his inscription read, "Happy Valentine's Day. Do you know the origins? The Romans believed that St. Valentine's Day was the day that all birds paired. This must be true since the two bald eagles perched together, near their nest site, just yesterday, February 13th. I love you—John."

He had spent the previous afternoon at the Blue Hill Library, looking up the origins of St. Valentine's Day. He was surprised when he came across the passage about the pairing of all birds on that one special day of the year. It gave him great pleasure to offer this wonderful pronouncement in my card. When he handed it to me, the look on his face is one I shall never forget: pure innocence, great joy, and deep love.

The snow is gone. The weather has turned warmer the last couple of days. While we had a short period of large, heavy snowflakes yesterday, it turned into a steady rain throughout the night. This morning, the landscape shows promise of better things to come. And if the groundhog was honest in yesterday's prediction, we will have an early spring. The warm rains have eased the vice-like handle along the cove, relaxing the shards and blocks of ice that unmercifully gripped the shoreline. Great ice blocks float into the center of the cove and drift, silently, into the reach. There must be a hundred or more pieces and jags of ice that have broken free, some smaller than others. Suddenly, dark shapes appear, pushing the cove's surface with their heads, bobbing bodies of black and white ducks surfacing along the ice blocks. The cove is now a study of black and white. I turn away for a moment; when I look back again, to my delight, the ducks have boarded the floating islands, like tiny life rafts, and they have hitched a ride into the reach. The cove is filled with sailing ducks.

Still, the nights are cold. I'm having difficulty sleeping, my heart heavier now, weighted by a dark and uncertain future. I feel chills run up and down my body. How I long to be warm again. I place my hand on John's chest and feel its soothing heat, but the comfort of his skin is quickly replaced by the uneasy rippling of his fasciculations, my hand rolling with his tremors, like a skiff atop a turbulent wave.

Quietly, so not to wake him, I slide out of bed and move toward the den. I flip the switch. Flooded with light, the room is teeming with wildlife. All around me are elephant families and great herds of buffalo. There are impala and graceful giraffes, zebra, and a rare black rhino. I stand alongside the framed photographs, lining the walls of the room, taken on our trip to South Africa. I lift my hand to the glass and gently press my fingertips onto the image of a sleek female leopard, moving effortlessly into a bramble of thorn. Closing my eyes, I let myself drift there. I am transported back into the bushveld, and I can smell, once again, the dry sweetness of the tall savannah grasses and, hidden within, the earthiness of the lion's golden coat. I feel the wonderful burn of a searing African sun across my bare shoulders, the tranquil sound of wing flaps from a saddle-billed stork cutting invisible shafts through a brilliant, blue sky. If only for a moment, my wakeful dream fills my once-heavy heart, now as light as a kingfisher's feather. Finally warm, I carry my hope with me, back to bed.

CHAPTER 7

Great Loves

Nothing happens unless first we dream.

~ Carl Sandburg

It was all Consi's fault. Our closest friend and neighbor in Maine, we spend countless hours with her after she departs from her home in Atlanta for her beloved cove-side cottage. John calls her Auntie Mame due to her flamboyant personality, generous spirit, bawdy good humor, and the ease at which she makes us feel. She is my dearest friend here, my confidant, and, in many ways, a surrogate mother. She and John tease each other mercilessly, and you would think they had known each other for a lifetime. Consi, to us, is the definition of extended family. She is family. Consi is also a consummate traveler. She had circumnavigated the globe and, even with her compromised health due to insulin-dependent diabetes and a cane, she travels to where her heart leads, hiking into the jungles of Angkor Wat, trekking orangutans in Borneo, or visiting wildlife sanctuaries in India. We are soulmates, she and I.

While I may have had a dreamer's love affair with Africa since childhood, it was Consi's doing that made the lifelong dream a reality. No longer was Africa a distant and unattainable fantasy but, upon traveling there, my life changed, and in ways I never imagined or may ever understand. If I thought, through the wanderlust eyes of an armchair traveler, that I would fall in love with Africa upon touching her soil, then my dreams were prophetic. But what I didn't know was that I would not only want to be a part of Africa, but I would need it, as surely and desperately as each breath of air. I suppose I shouldn't have been all that surprised. But, on arrival, and for the first time, I knew my life would never be the same, and Africa, indelibly, would become my greatest source of inspiration.

Perhaps knowing that John was ill — although at the time we were a few months from the final diagnosis of terminal disease — I knew I had to shift footing, the crushing blow of losing John, my anchor and very core, fast becoming a frightening possibility. If that were true, and if John was dying, then somehow Africa gently eased her way in, never allowing my center to become empty, void of dreams, and tethering me to a hopeful future.

It is an oddly wonderful thing to love something so deeply, a mysterious place you do not know nor have ever been. But maybe I did know Africa as well as we can know anything or anyone we fall hopelessly and passionately in love with. It comes from a small corner of the heart, an infinitesimal spot reserved for great loves. Why we love is one of life's great mysteries. My heart blossomed the moment I first saw John. It blossomed again in a similar fashion — like a first, great love — when I set foot in Africa. And, as I would find out, it was indeed as real and as profound as anything I have ever known.

During the final months of medical testing, and more trips to Boston hospitals than we would have liked, we were fast burning out. Most maladies had been ruled out, and ALS loomed heavy on our minds. One evening, Consi asked us to stop in for a drink. She seemed excited and wanted to talk to us about something. "I have a great idea," she said, once we settled down with glasses of wine. "Let's all go to Africa." We laughed, not sure if she was serious, but she knew we were tired, of both mind and body, and it was painfully apparent that

John's symptoms were becoming worse. Consi, concerned and believing that travel is a cure for all ills, thought a trip would be highly beneficial. "Look," she said, "I have traveled all over the world with the exception of Africa. You know I have always wanted to go, and I know how much you've always wanted to go. Since I cannot do that kind of travel alone, if you will go with me, help me and my stick along, I will pay for most of the trip." It was an unbelievably generous offer.

In her 60s, Consi's health was questionable because of her diabetes, her inability to walk and steady herself, her dependence on a cane. For us, money was the issue; we didn't think we could afford to go for the five weeks she proposed, but she wouldn't have it any other way. Initially, we said no, we couldn't accept that kind of a gift; it was much too generous and made us a bit uncomfortable. But when she convinced us that she could not do the trip otherwise, a dream would be lost, and couldn't think of anyone she would rather see Africa with, we agreed to go. She extended the generous invitation to another one of her friends as well, so if John and I needed time alone, she would have the company of Rennie, a familiar traveling companion. It seemed ideal.

So, amid the turmoil that had defined much of our lives the last year, Consi's gift of Africa was unlike any other. An unexpected and much-needed escape from the burden of pressing health issues, it was a dream of a lifetime, a dream come true. The trip to South Africa transformed our lives and, being an introduction to the continent for both John and me, together, it was a great adventure and life-affirming journey. We felt truly alive again for the first time in many, many months, and overwhelmed with joy and emotion. The foreboding darkness that had shrouded our spirits had suddenly lifted, and we remembered what it was like to experience everything fresh and new again, much like a child does when seeing the ocean for the first time. There are few things in life that can inspire such awe. We were surrounded by and overflowing with it for five glorious weeks.

CHAPTER 8

Africa

... Something has happened here, is happening,
will happen — whole landscapes seem alert.

~ Peter Matthiessen

If Africa is a tall tale, then surely the bush and its miraculous life forms are a song, a poem. How can one look onto the massive swirl of limbs that is the baobab tree and not hear music? Can one watch the tenderness of a mother elephant caressing her calf and not find perfect poetry in her motions?

I kept a journal of this first, great adventure. It's because of this journey, these singular and life-changing experiences, that John and I have been able to cope with much of the chaos now encompassing our lives. When we get frightened or overwhelmed, we pull out our "safety net" — the videotapes and photographs that remind us of better days, days of Africa. We admire the intricate weave and beauty of the Zulu baskets that adorn our tabletops; run our fingers over the cool, smooth finish of stone-carved animals. For me, there hasn't been a day since our return that my mind has not drifted there — across her endless plains, sweet remembrance of the beauty and generosity of her people. We found a part of ourselves there. I know I will go back. I have to, for I left a part of myself in return.

South Africa, 1998 ~ only a few years after the dismantling of apartheid, culminating on April 27, 1994, when the first democratic elections were held in South Africa, with people of all races being able to vote.

After two nights in the capital of Pretoria, not far from Johannesburg, we decide to leave a day early. The city, although beautiful, has a stifling feel to it—unseen but palpable. There is an undercurrent of tension and, from what we sense, paranoia. Hotel management warns us not to walk around most parts of the city, even during daylight hours. Never be on the street at night. Avoid certain neighborhoods altogether. Hold valuables close to the body. Be aware. We are mindful and careful, not naïve, and yet have done what we've wanted: visited the wonderful Kruger bird museum, eaten at restaurants regardless of neighborhood, spent time at the cheetah breeding center. It's time to move on.

We load our rental car, bursting at the seams with Consi's excessive luggage (a woman who, afraid that it might not be available in South Africa, has transported halfway around the globe three jumbo containers of Hellmann's mayonnaise, one of her staples), and head for Kruger National Park. We have raised more than a few eyebrows with our plan to drive ourselves around South Africa and through Swaziland for five-plus weeks. We are often reminded that the roads may be dangerous, crime is rife, carjacking is rampant, not to mention the remote areas where we'll be traveling with roads, if they exist, treacherously potholed and precarious. We have done our homework, however, which is the best one can do before travel, and feel safe enough with the four of us in the car and our routes well mapped out. The rest is out of our control.

It has only been four years since the fall of apartheid in 1994, and the country is just now seeing a boom in the tourism industry. That said, there is no doubt that South Africa is still in the midst of turmoil. The widespread poverty suffered by the majority of its people is painfully apparent. From what we read beforehand and have experienced in just a few days, a few white South Africans are still feeling a bit threatened, if not paranoid, with a long history of white supremacy coming to an end. They are shocked, perhaps, that the end of apartheid came peacefully; that a violent uprising against them by the oppressed and often brutalized blacks was not their fate, the fate of South Africa. We may be mistaken but, in part, it seems that much of their fear is of their own creation. Paranoia cuts deep. All of the raised eyebrows regarding our decision to drive ourselves around the country, and the barrage of cautionary tales in Pretoria, have come from older whites. It may be some time before these very people feel safe within the confines of their own hearts and minds. A prison of the mind and heart can oftentimes feel far more oppressive than bars and wire.

So, today, John is at the wheel. He is up for the challenge of driving through the South African countryside, apparently comfortable with the transportation reversals—managing the steering wheel on the right side of the car and driving on the opposite side of the road—and the three women with three maps and countless opinions, acting as navigators. He is a brave man.

We take a leisurely route, winding through the breathtaking Mpumalanga region. After a few days of being surrounded by the magnificent, sculpted cliffs of the Drakensberg Escarpment, immense waterfalls, and Grand Canyon-like gorges of God's Window and Blyde River Canyon, we cross into Kruger

National Park en route to our bushcamp, Bateleur, named after the grand eagle, and in the far northern regions of the reserve. We've been in the park only a few minutes before the roadsides are filled with giraffe, elephant, zebra and impala. Ecstatic is a mild expression for the first, and sudden, encounter of these magnificent animals in the wild, and surprised at how it takes a moment to fully register that these wonderful creatures are roaming alongside us and in the roadway. It's not often that one stops for an elephant in the middle of the road. Or, rather than yielding for oncoming traffic, slows to make way for a herd of zebra in no apparent hurry to move through an intersection.

Halfway to Bateleur, we stop for lunch at Mopani camp. Below the camp is a vast marshland, crystalline lake pools filled with elephant and hippo. Overlooking the marsh and its spongy banks, grand fish eagles perch on dead tree branches. Kingfishers sing their distinctive buzz and trill-like song, fluttering then dipping from branch to puddle like huge dragonflies. The searing midday sun causes a hazy, rippling effect, making the land move like slow water. Unfamiliar bird sounds pierce the air while raptors cut wide, graceful circles in the sky.

With the first pale blush of morning light, we prepare for the 5:30 bush drive with our young guide, Neels van Wyk. From the open Land Rover, we are greeted by a sunrise of soft pastel ribbons lifting above the bushveld. Stopping along an elevated riverbed, we alight from the vehicle to get a closer look at the crocodile-filled waters. Unwary shorebirds drink from the river;

the beautiful heron, plovers, and cranes seem unaware of the crocodile's proximity. Later, we are privileged to see the rare saddle-billed stork in flight. Neels investigates fresh lion tracks moving northward along a narrow, dry riverbed.

By 9 o'clock, I'm at the blind or hide where I sit, mesmerized, and taking notes, until well past noon. As I sit, hidden from sight, a large herd of impala comes to drink, including a small juvenile with what appears to be a huge bite wound on its side. The wound is fresh and raw. Neels says it was probably attacked by hyena and lucky to escape. You don't get many second chances in nature.

After dinner, John and I head back to the blind. The warm wind is blowing hard, whipping leaves and branches and making the animals at the waterhole nervous. Another impala family — mother, father, and juvenile — carefully make their way toward the small drinking pool. It's been a hot day, close to 100 degrees, and they're thirsty. They're also extremely skittish as the intense winds are making it difficult to scent the air around them. Without being able to smell from which direction a predator is approaching, the impala are left vulnerable. We sit in silence for over two hours watching this family gingerly make their way to the waterhole, then run back, repeating this sad spectacle over and over again. At times, they get within a few inches of drinking, only to be frightened away once more. The baby impala, tired of the back and forth, lies down not far from its parents and within the small shadow of a tree. It's difficult to watch this family, obviously frightened and yet very thirsty, get so close to drinking only to repeatedly retreat. If they don't drink here tonight, they will probably not have water until daybreak. In the two hours at the blind, the family never took a single sip. Finally, the exhausted impala give up and move into the safer confines of shadows and trees. Within moments three hyenas appear, taking long, leisurely drinks from the waterhole. Satiated, they enjoy a cool, refreshing swim while the others stay motionless in the shadowy distance. I could sit here all night, waiting for the mysterious unfolding of nocturnal events. With the winds howling and temperatures dropping, John heads back to camp, a star-lit sky illuminating his path. I have to stay just awhile longer. There is no interlude in the drama of nature, and I can't bear to miss any of its performance.

The landscape around Bateleur is peppered with trees — from massive, thousand-year-old baobabs with their gnarled and twisted limbs, to the ubiquitous umbrella thorn and its wide, flat canopy, and the equally as lovely mopane, teak, and nyala trees. A crocodile rests on the warm dam wall while two others swim lazily below. Nighthawks — like huge, nocturnal butterflies — flit through the air. Scrub hares, long-tailed shrikes, dwarf mongoose, herons, and a porcupine move about the path, either winding down their day's routine or just beginning at nightfall. A spotted eagle-owl, a herd of impala, and a baboon family all exist around our rolling vehicle as we permeate the violet evening. As John holds me near, I look into a star-studded sky with the backdrop of ancient trees silhouetted against cobalt blue and silver lights, and cannot believe I am here. This is Africa, far more beautiful than any dream.

The following evening, as we prepare for another night drive with Neels, Consi decides to stay back at camp. Neels is aware of Consi's lack of mobility and dependence on a cane, which has limited places where he can take us on foot. So, at the last minute, he decides to take John, Rennie, and me on a different journey through the bush. Our first stop is the dam where he leads us on foot across the expanse of the dam wall. All of 3 feet wide, with no railing, and with a nearly 30-foot drop on either side, we carefully navigate the lip of the dam with the setting sun on our backs, crocodiles below. Just to the left, fish eagles perch in nearby trees. Dikkops, water birds, impala, a waterbuck, and Egyptian geese all feed and drink in the pools below. To the right, over 20 crocodiles languidly swim in the cool, dark waters. At the far end of the dam wall, cupped in the tranquil, final stages of daylight and warmth, rests a large baboon troop enjoying the last fingers of the sun before scrambling down to the safety and confines of the nyala trees. At dusk, this seems to be the gathering place for all creatures. Feeling intoxicated by the wonderful assault on our senses, we leave this magical spot where the synergy of sunlight and water converges, and all creatures great and small congregate within its life force.

As if this experience alone was not worthy of a lifetime of memories, Neels offers to take us to another of his favorite spots so we can bear witness to the "best of African sunsets." At the Lookout, we clamor across ancient boulders, hiking to an outcropping of massive rock formations high above the

African landscape. The day before, Neels had spotted a young leopard sunning himself on the rock ledge. Stretching below us and as far as the eye can see, miles and miles of untouched African bushveld, the golden light of the setting sun casting an incandescent flush across the canopy of a thousand trees. The sun, burning crimson, dips below a melting horizon and to the left of a darkening tree silhouette, making the tree look as if it's ablaze. Quietly, the three-quarter moon rises behind us into a fluid, indigo sky.

Later that night, I awaken to the distant roar of lions. I gaze out my open window at one particularly bright star. I am in Africa.

We rise early as we must leave Bateleur for our next destination, Talamati bushcamp, in the southern region of the park. Before we leave, and as John has done each morning, he gathers dead moths from our bedroom floor and carries them to the verandah to scatter beneath the birdbath. The yellow hornbills have become especially fond of John—from low tree branches, they await his early-morning offerings, as do the iridescent grackles, blue waxbills, and the lourie (or the "go-away bird," as South Africans call them, due to their sometimes loud and obnoxious whine).

At Talamati near sunset, the sky turns ominous shades of gray and black with ribbons of blood red and cobalt blue. Thunder rumbles and heat lightning flashes both vertically and horizontally, shattering the sky into a million crystals; then, mild rain. As quickly as the rain falls, it stops, the air becoming thick and sticky once again.

After last night's rain at Talamati, miniature 1-inch toads began to appear. Springing out of the moist grass, they hopped by the dozens onto the walkway below our tiled verandah, looking like an olive-green river of toads.

Africa is not for the faint of heart. Seldom does one experience subtlety. Everything here is extreme, dramatic: the veld, the vast mountains and gorges, powerful thunder and light shows, searing heat, an infinite sky, and the rarity of animal and plant life that exists nowhere else on the Earth. Every sight, every breath is a new and exciting experience. The lore, beauty, and mystery that one lusts after in dreaming of Africa are even more intense and spectacular upon arrival. On a warm night, with only a hint of a breeze, you begin to smell animal scents riding on the wind.

I know that nothing will be the same for me upon arriving back home. This experience, Africa, is life changing and will surely make most other things seem dull in comparison. Will my life in Maine have lost some of its sharpness, its color? Will I be as excited over the ebb and flow of the tide, the song of the chickadee, the nesting bald eagles, as I once was, before Africa? This magical place makes those singular moments, once so rewarding and rich, seem muted now.

How can one retain the initial excitement over the small things and the gifts of day to day after witnessing a herd of elephants, a thousand storks in flight, the eyes of a bull giraffe upon you? Maybe it's simply the small gifts we daily receive from nature that enrich our lives, incrementally. Perhaps the big adventures—the "Africa's"—add the spice, the counterbalance, making the shades and colors of life, past and present, all the brighter, more in focus. Whatever the answer, if any, I feel different now, changed. After less than two weeks, I feel as though I have ingested a lifetime of living through my senses alone. I've never felt so alive.

I hope, on some cold, winter night in Maine, I can close my eyes and smell the impala at the waterhole, see the impossible iridescent colors of the bee-eater, feel the heat of the African sun burning across my shoulders.

Cornell, our new guide at Talamati, will lead tonight's safari. Only minutes into the bush, we spot a small herd of buffalo including a mother with her hour's-old calf. Then, suddenly, our first lion! In the fading afternoon light, a lone female saunters across the dirt path, her belly bloated and hanging low to the ground, and disappears into the tall savannah grasses. Cornell determines that she is ready to give birth within a few days. A lioness will leave the pride to give birth in solitude, only introducing her cubs when they are a few days or weeks old.

As the night envelopes, we see the glowing red eyes of diminutive bushbabies hiding in trees and peering out of hollows, a solitary steenbok; near the dam, another herd of buffalo. As Cornell drives closer toward the herd, we are suddenly aware of a pride of seven lions lurking nearby. The light is rapidly fading, but we can see the clear outline of the lounging figures, well camouflaged in the swaying golden grasses. As dark blue turns to black night, only the illuminated red eyes caught in the handheld torchlight reveal the lions moving closer to the unsuspecting herd of buffalo. Silently, and in hunkered motion, they move in, scouting out the weakest in the herd, and by all indications, a kill is imminent. We choose not to stay and witness the kill; a buffalo taken by lions is never a quick and easy death but rather a bloody and prolonged battle. It is the way of nature, certainly, but, for tonight, the decision is unanimous to move on, not to witness or interfere with the life-and-death struggle about to unfold.

As we near the end of our journey, a massive herd of buffalo moves across the plain and ambles into the road, directly in front of our Land Rover. Land Rovers in South Africa are open sided, no windows, no protective glass, nothing between you and the wild. The buffalo are within feet of us now, well over a hundred head, many snorting and grunting at the intrusion of the vehicle. We will be going nowhere fast, and Cornell turns off the engine as we sit quietly, very quietly, surrounded by the great herd. It's a dreamlike vision being enclosed by the darkened shapes of these immense creatures with their strong, powerful bodies; thick heads and necks; flaring, moist nostrils; and, not least of all, threatening horns at chest level and the overwhelming primal sense of vulnerability. The smell of the herd sits heavy on the still, night air—randy and gamy but not unpleasant. We sit motionless for what seems a lifetime, barely breathing as the herd relaxes and slowly begins to move away from the vehicle. Of the Big Five, as they are referred to in Africa—lion, leopard, buffalo, elephant, and rhino—the buffalo is the most feared.

Extremely cunning and dangerous, every precaution must be taken so as not to provoke them in any way. More people are killed or injured by buffalo, particularly a lone bull, than by any other of the Big Five.

Next morning reveals a lion kill. Three young lions have just finished feasting on their prey while hundreds of vultures crowd the ground and nearby tree limbs, looking as if they'll snap from the weight of so many scavengers. Into the mix and looking for entrails come a handful of black-backed jackals. Semihidden beneath scrub, and just to my left, one of the lions rests alongside the buffalo remains, guarding the kill. Through the bramble, and not 10 feet away, I see the lovely, young face of the lion, golden brown and unblemished. His paws are outstretched before him, huge and strong. The carcass is half eaten, the stench of death wafting on the warm morning breeze. All that remains of the buffalo is its head and shoulders. Its eyes are shut, mouth partially opened, teeth bared in one last snarl before death seized. The lion rests his head atop the buffalo's, like a flesh-and-bone pillow, its head nuzzled against the snout and teeth of its dead prey. The lion, satiated, is now sleepy and full. His formidable paws gently nudge the side of the carcass, bits of flesh and blood, exposed ribs. I cannot get out of my mind the buffalo's last expression before death. I avert my eyes but see it clearly. I look again. This time, the lion looks up, tired, bloated and relaxed, and, for a moment, I meet the fluid gaze of his tawny eyes. Our eyes lock; then, quickly, I look away.

We bid farewell to Kruger and head toward Notten's bushcamp, just a short drive outside of the park. Notten's—a small, family-owned game lodge—is located within the famed Sabie Sand Game Reserve, abutting Kruger Park. There are no fences between Kruger and the Sabie Sand, and animals roam freely to and from the park and the neighboring reserves.

Tonight, for the first time, we see the elusive and endangered white rhino. Halfway through our game-spotting, Tom, our guide, stops the vehicle so we can watch the moon rising off the horizon. A night bird cries out somewhere in the distance. Beneath the brilliant light of a near full moon, we marvel at the Southern Cross constellation, as illuminated ribbons streak the sky. Secretly, I make a wish, for John to remain healthy for as long as possible, and one day to return to Africa.

At night, to stand beneath the vast African sky, I feel a part of the whole, the landscape, the grasses and trees, animals and stars. For that brief moment, I have a better understanding of the interconnectedness of all creatures, all life forms, soil and leaf. There is symmetry here. A symbiosis of sorts that, when perfect, when it works, makes all seem well with the universe. And so, for tonight, this moment, I will hold onto the dream that all wishes can come true, no matter how difficult to believe. If anywhere I can believe, it is here, wrapped in John's arms, and around us still, Africa's nurturing embrace.

The early morning, tender pink, is warm with a light breeze. We roll into the bush with the two Toms—our driver/guide and our tracker from a local ethnic group. He sits atop the hood of the Land Rover, a shotgun strapped across his broad shoulders at all times. Although young, he is an expert at his craft, having learned from his father, and his father before him. Within moments, he spots fresh lion and leopard prints. We drive slowly down the road to find a beautiful female leopard casually strolling along the path, the morning light glistening across her back. She is nothing short of remarkable and, to me, the loveliest of all the big cats. She is smaller than I expected but solidly built. Tom says she looks to be barely three years old. We follow her for a while, then stop, turning off the motor, sitting quietly and observing. Suddenly, she turns away from the bush and calmly moves toward the vehicle, stopping not 2 feet away from where I sit.

Her coat is a masterpiece; her eyes, pale topaz, melting into the warm hues of her sleek, velvety body. I cannot believe she is so close. If I stretched out my arm, I could brush the top of her tawny head. And, just as suddenly as she approached, she is off, her huge, padded feet and agile body moving effortlessly, like liquid gold, into the bush. She senses something, hears the faintest noise. She doesn't make a sound in her movements, not a twig or blade of grass is snapped or disturbed. She has spotted a duiker, a small antelope, hidden somewhere in the scrub. It gets away. This time.

Tonight offers the biggest thrill yet of our bush experiences, and maybe the most frightening. At dusk, Tom drives us onto an immense plain of tall grasses and few trees. In the middle of this vastness stands a lone, female buffalo with her days-old calf. Tom reports that she has been separated from the herd, exhausted after recently giving birth and unable to keep up. The vision of mother and calf, alone, and swallowed by the darkening expanse of landscape is heartbreaking. She no longer has the strength in numbers from her herd to protect her and her newborn calf. Her calf will be an easy target tonight for both lion and hyena. The mother will be on her own to defend her young, and, more than likely, will also fall prey. Tom stops the Land Rover and, in hushed silence, we watch the mother and calf slowly walk away from us.

Abruptly, the mother turns around and starts moving toward the vehicle at a much quicker pace, her baby trotting alongside. Before we know what is happening, she charges the vehicle, her massive head and horns bent down and at chest level of where I am seated. Immediately, Tom begins to pound his fists into the hood of the vehicle in an attempt to divert her attention. Alarmed, a fellow passenger screams for Tom to shoot—although this is not, and should not be, an option. We are the intruders here. That said, it's terribly frightening. We are in an open-sided vehicle, and I'm not far from the immense horns and girth of this protective mother. A female cape buffalo can weigh in at approximately 1,200 pounds and will go to extremes to protect her young. As Tom continues to slam the hood and yell, I quickly slide to the center of the seat. Again, a second charge, then a third! The vehicle rocks with each slam of her head, teetering precariously just as Tom is able to get the vehicle started. It's all happening so quickly that responding seems suspended in midair. Finally, with his foot to the gas, Tom quickly backs up and onto the dirt road. For a split second, it looks as though she will charge yet again. But, at the last moment, she turns, looking back only briefly. Then, with baby in tow, she walks away as the darkness deepens and night begins to fall.

I can still see her and her tiny calf trotting across that lonely and barren plain, disappearing into blackness; her baby's chance of survival, bleak. This lone, female buffalo was overly protective because she alone was left to care for and defend her young. I can only hope that they made it through the night. But nights, here, are never left to chance.

Heading toward Ndumo wilderness camp in a remote corner of South Africa bordering Mozambique.

Ndumo proves to be a much longer drive than we anticipated. We stop for gas in Jozini, a small, meager-looking village, tucked high in the mountains and alongside a massive dam. The scenery is lush and fertile, the locals friendly, but the facilities and housing are reflective of a poverty-stricken community. A remote village, it's apparent that the locals manage with very little. It's market day, and tables and stalls line the only road through town. It is hot and dusty, and people are selling their wares — everything from piles of used clothing to miscellaneous meats, chickens, and produce, all hanging from wooden rafters or splayed across the ground atop colorful cloths and blankets. The late-morning sun is beating down upon the mysterious cuts of raw meat, and already the smell of flesh is permeating the mountain air. A group of children, riding in the back of an old, rusty pickup truck, wave and smile broadly, shouting "Hello!" as we pull into the only gas station in town. Luckily, we are able to refuel as we're told that this station usually runs out of petrol by midday, and there is no other station around for miles.

Jozini is a squatter's town, and the inhabitants, like so many others in remote villages, have few options, if any, for long-distance transportation. These people are self-sufficient, fending for themselves as they always have. But life is anything but easy here and, regardless of all the smiling faces, they look worn and haggard from making do.

Ndumo is still many kilometers away and the roads and mountain passes are horribly potholed, making travel slow and precarious. As John maneuvers his way around the potholes, our car dropping and jolting at every one, we are amazed at the response we get from so many children along the roadsides. Most of the children are wearing uniforms, on their way to and from school. This is a promising sight, especially in such a poor, rural village, and, from what we have seen, the schools are oftentimes many miles away. The scores of children, always barefoot, wave and wave as we slowly drive by. Some of the smaller ones jump up and down — the excitement, perhaps, at seeing a vehicle, strangers, someone from the outside and different. But, whatever the reason, they flash wide, beautiful smiles as we pass. The older children offer us thumbs-up, a hundred times over and better still, additional nonstop grins, the most honest smiles I have ever seen.

The poverty, though, is sobering. And, while perhaps not surprising, it is nonetheless shocking to see firsthand. Many black South African families live on less than $2 a day. It is one thing to read about poverty, to see still images or television reports, but to witness the dire conditions in which so many people live and survive is a much-needed dose of reality. Many of the houses en route to Ndumo are nothing more than simple shelters, wooden shacks with loose, thatched roofs, some more basic or makeshift than others. A few roofs are pieces of corrugated sheet metal, sitting atop the structures, unfastened. Other houses appear to be single-room cement block, most without glass for windows, if windows exist at all. Often, clothing, towels, torn pieces of cloth are tacked up as curtains or used as doors, acting as barriers against the elements. Cows, donkeys, and goats line the roadways and shuffle into the middle, in no hurry to move. As we crawl down the road at a snail's pace, I see John's somber expression as he peers one last time into the rear-view mirror, our car kicking up clouds of dust, blurring the vision of children and livestock.

After hours on the road, we arrive at Ndumo. A lovely lake, teeming with wildlife, glistens in the late-afternoon sun. Massive, pale-green fig and fever trees line our path—huge girths and twisted limbs, more like living sculptures casting shadows and lightshards through leaves and branches. Birdsong and the incessant trill of frogs are everywhere. Cranes, herons, plovers, and iridescent kingfishers drink at the lake and smaller ponds; crocodiles rest lazily along the soft banks; hippos rise and spout in the emerald-green waters.

The camp—huge tents on stilts with winding, teakwood paths and decks—rises above the fertile ground and pan, or floodplain. Our tent is perhaps 10 to 15 feet above the marshy, jungle-like floor that is home to a monitor lizard or two, and overhead a dense canopy of trees ornamented with delicate weaver bird nests. Our small deck juts over the Banzi Pan floodplain, filled with crocodiles and waterfowl.

Later that afternoon, our guide, Trevor, takes us for a hike on the opposite side of the Banzi Pan. While crocodiles bask in the nearby waters, a huge male hippo is not pleased with the intrusion and loudly grunts his displeasure. You don't fool around with hippos; they can be extremely dangerous, and, for all their bulk and squat stature, they are much quicker on their feet than one might imagine. An adult hippo can weigh well over 3,000 pounds and charge at close to 20 miles per hour on dry land. Trevor warns us, should a hippo charge, to run for the nearest tree and climb as fast as possible. John and I look at one another and smile, knowing full well that if this were to happen, he'd better pray for wings as he'd never make it up a tree. The ground here too is difficult to negotiate as it's waterlogged, spongy due to its closeness to the pan. With every step, mud and ooze rise above our shoes as we sink into the primordial muck.

I'm enveloped by prehistoric bird cries and massive wingspans cutting through moist air; dense, jungle-like thicket abutting the pan; and flashes of light moving through ancient, gnarled limbs. There is no sign of modern-day life, only the potent smells of brackish water and reeds; wet grasses; dripping leaves and moss; wet, rich soil; and animal scents heavy on the wind.

Leaving Ndumo, and in order to reach our next destination along the coast, we drive through the landlocked Kingdom of Swaziland, a diminutive country of both savannah and rain forest, and vast plantations of sugar cane and citrus. We stop for a few days in the capital of Mbabane before continuing onto Rocktail Bay wilderness camp on the Indian Ocean. Rocktail Bay is remote and untouched; pristine, white-sand beaches; no one around for miles. The glistening beach is desolate with the exception of gulls and sand crabs darting in and out of the turquoise surf. This lovely stretch of sand wraps around a small arc of a bay, dunes rising and falling with an unexpected backdrop of dense forest. This is a place where endangered turtles come to lay and hatch their eggs; no intrusion of vehicles or crowds, only footprints in the sand. The water is warm yet refreshing, and John and I have an invigorating swim, then a leisurely stroll along the shoreline, collecting shells and enjoying this beautiful paradise to ourselves.

After dinner on the verandah and under the now ubiquitous African thatched roof, the resident thick-tailed bushbaby,

Gremlin, arrives on schedule. He first appeared some five years ago, eating sugar and anything sweet left on tables. Now, he shows up each evening for a dose of human company and the treat of a banana. He allows the staff to hold him as he has become rather tame, seems comfortable being handed over to me. He scrambles to my shoulder, allowing me to hold him, gently nibbling on my fingers as I scratch his ears and stroke his stomach, a favorite spot. A primate and part of the lemur family, bushbabies are beautiful, nocturnal animals with huge, black eyes and dense, velvety fur. They look more like a koala bear than a primate.

I set off for the beach early next morning, walking on planked paths threaded through forest and to the dunes. It is hot and windy. Except for me, the beach lies empty. It's just me and the crashing surf, hot sun, and tiny crabs and sand spiders darting in and out of their burrows. How good it feels to be alone—alone with the sea and sky. I need this time, however brief, to think and to reflect. While this trip has been a wonderful distraction, there is no real escaping the illness that plagues John. Neither the biblical sunsets nor warm, ocean waters can make it go away. He fatigues easily, I have noticed a slight limp, and the fasciculations have spread to his chest and neck. I have tried not to worry too much about it, but it finds a way of creeping into my thoughts at each waking moment. How can it not?

Three young African boys appear along the beach below me, fishing in the crashing surf. Two of them have poles; the other is holding what looks to be a wooden club. I see him fling the club upon the sand, again and again. I can only assume he is delivering a fatal blow to a caught fish.

Before sunset, when the sharks come toward shore, John gets one last swim in the soothing waters of the Indian Ocean. The warm saltwater seems to ease his nagging pain, relax his muscles. From my spot on the beach, I watch him make his way to the sea like a young boy all too eager to lose himself in the rolling waves. I watch him disappear into the crystalline waters. For a time, his world is nothing more than the therapeutic feel of an ocean embracing his body, the ripple of waves massaging his shoulders, the embryonic rocking by a form primordial.

On this overdiscovered and overexploited earth the sea remains a wilderness, a resource not of goods but of what is rich and wild. That which we have been unable to use up, or harry into extinction, has the power to renew. The sea is a positive mystery. I hear the surf's continual breathing in the distance; I see the stars that literally cover the sky over the beach on a winter's night like white animal plankton in the spring waters; and I realize that I know more about them than I know about myself. The depths are still ahead, with the fear and the temptation that the undiscovered arouses in us.

~ John Hay, *The Great Beach*

CHAPTER 9

A Surreal Meal and Other Bites

It's not that I'm afraid to die. I just don't want to be there when it happens.

~ Woody Allen

Home for a few months now, John continues to work. We moved to Maine with a plan to live a more frugal life, one of self-sufficiency, and only work sparingly outside of the home. With the sale of our small San Francisco flat, and if we were careful and prudent with our finances, we would be allowed a bit more freedom from the arduous work week to which we had been accustomed. The move afforded me more time and creative energy to write, and days closer to nature. Within a short time, however, John became bored. After all, he was a healthy and capable 43-year-old, still eager to learn and apply himself in new ways. In the city, he had worked in finance, including as partner-owner of a video, film, and communications firm, handling the financial aspects of running a small business.

What whetted his appetite now, though, was the thought of creatively working with his hands. He had loved the remodeling process of our flat in San Francisco and, not long after settling in Maine, hooked up with a few carpentry teams to build houses. He loved manual labor and the rewards of seeing something tangible before him. The pay was low and the hours long, but, as John loved to say, "That's the way it is—I'm the low man on the scrotum pole," a saying he coined for a beginner on any job.

Once he became adept at being a part of a home-building crew, he offered his services to Habitat for Humanity and spent many Saturdays helping to build homes for families in need. He was immersing himself in our new lifestyle, and he loved being part of a small community. Before long, he was on the board of directors of the Historical Society and treasurer of our local library. He was in his element, even if spreading himself a bit too thin.

What has helped in keeping John's spirits high is the concern and flexibility that work crews have afforded him. When his symptoms began, and the barrage of doctor appointments and trips to Boston hospitals became a routine part of our lives, John worried about his lack of work time and inefficiency on the job. He has been, and will forever be, grateful to his good friend, Dave, a master carpenter and builder, who has hired John to work on most of his crews. Dave has eased John's mind by offering him work that accommodates his capabilities. He has comforted John with the knowledge that his work and his presence on each job are still greatly appreciated and valuable, and he has not hesitated to give him time off when we've needed to take care of pressing medical issues. When John began a temporary, trial-drug therapy and would wake up each morning groggy and out of sorts, Dave would simply say, "Get here when you get here," and that was that.

A few weeks ago, I got a call late morning. It was Dave, calling from the local hospital emergency room. John had cut through his thumb using a table saw at the job site and had lost a lot of blood. It was an accident waiting to happen. It was his right hand, which by then had already lost much of its muscle mass and strength. He continued to work, although increasingly tired and in pain, not yet willing to admit that his capabilities were diminishing and might eventually prove dangerous.

It was a learning experience. After stitches and time spent with a hand surgeon in Ellsworth, John was told he wouldn't be able to work for at least a month. More than anything, or so he said, he was unnerved at having his first-ever stitch. But, as time wore on, he realized the profound meaning of the accident, as did Dave. It was time to make adjustments — "another wake-up call," as John finally admitted. His ability had been compromised and, therefore, his duties and responsibilities accordingly. He continues to be part of Dave's crew, albeit taking on less physically challenging roles. He fatigues easily now and works on a part-time basis. But Dave continues to keep him on — not out of pity but to tackle the smaller jobs that others may not have time for: the picking up of supplies and, not the least of all, keeping the crew laughing. He also has John looking after the books or finances for most of his jobs, something John knows and enjoys. I cannot ask him to stop working nor would I want to. It keeps him going, feeling needed, feeling alive. It keeps his mind and body occupied and, during that time, miles away from the reality of illness that pulses throughout his failing limbs.

Once, while recuperating from his injured thumb, John said that not working made him re-evaluate who he was. He said that many men tend to define themselves by their jobs and professions, what they "do" to earn a living. If he could not work, would he feel a sense of loss about who he was? Would he feel less somehow, insignificant? Would he feel as though the disease was now defining him as a person, defining his capabilities or loss thereof? He struggled with this for some time before admitting what he knew all along: What we see in another human being and how we define others should not be based on "what we do" in life to "earn" a living. Our jobs represent only a minute part of whom and what we are. How many times at parties, other social gatherings or events, the first question a stranger asks is, "And what do you do?" Now, John likes to say, "What needs to be done?" Better still, "What did you have in mind?" That one always makes him laugh and raises the occasional eyebrow.

Dealing with disease can be a very lonely place. Unless you have been there yourself, it's difficult to truly understand the depth of the psychological dynamics at play. At times, while talking with my friends, I can sense their inability to comprehend. They can empathize and lend a caring ear, which may be enough for that moment, but, for the most part, we are vastly separated by circumstance. Only to a certain extent can they imagine what it means to have a spouse diagnosed with terminal disease. They can try to imagine their lives without their loved ones, pushing a wheelchair, the nightmare of watching a spouse suffer, the loss of their youth or lightness of being, but they cannot truly understand. It is far too surreal.

The aloneness too comes from the lack of acknowledgement from others as to your well-being. I won't say their lack of concern, but rather their initial thought and gesture are always to inquire about the one who is ill. But there is a void, an emptiness that overshadows you when no one asks how you are doing, how you are coping. Once in a while, I need someone to ask, "How are you handling all of this?" or simply, "Are you okay?" Those few words would mean the world. They would provide a Band-Aid, no matter how small, to protect the open wound. For the most part, however, people don't realize how the spouse of a terminally ill person suffers too. There are few fates worse than seeing the person you love most in life dealing with terminal illness. There are many times that I would gladly take on John's disease, just to save him from all the suffering, all the despair. Most days, my life is not fun and games. It is not light or easy, and any thoughts of free-spiritedness are long gone, shadows of another life. Just once in a while, I would cherish the thought of someone, anyone, asking how I am. Then, for a short time, I would not feel so alone.

The doors are beginning to open, bit by bit. While we have discussed many aspects of John having ALS and what it all means, there are a few topics so formidable that we have crept around them, pushing them further and further into darkened corners. The other evening during dinner, these topics easily surfaced. For whatever reason, we were feeling strong at that moment and ready to broach aspects of the disease that had previously and deliberately not been discussed. We talked about our greatest fears, what frightened us the most as the disease progressed. To make the topic lighter, to ease into it, we played a game of sorts. I asked John what frightened him the most. "Being in a wheelchair," he answered quickly, "and you having to take care of me in a wheelchair. I know what that is like having taken care of my mother, and I don't want that burden put on you."

This surprised me. But what surprised me even more was when I asked him what he thought I was most fearful of. "Being alone, being left alone in Maine without your family and friends." This shocked me further still as that was perhaps the least of my worries and fears. "I'm not afraid of being alone," I said softly. "I'm afraid of being without you. Those are two very different things." I paused and, when I caught my breath, I said, "And the thought of you in a wheelchair and my caring for you in a chair is not particularly frightening to me. I can deal with that, with you being paralyzed." "So what does scare you, more than anything else, truthfully?" he asked. This time, I took an even deeper breath and knew that now was the time for honesty. "It's you not being able to speak," I whispered. "I can't imagine never hearing your voice again." He nodded reassuringly as his eyes met mine. "That's a long way off," he smiled. But there were no other words to assuage that fear for either of us. We continued with our meal in a mutual, silent acknowledgment that the discussion was over. For now, we had bitten off all that we could chew.

CHAPTER 10

A Hummingbird's Tale

... to listen to stars and birds ...
this is to be my symphony.

~ William Henry Channing

This past summer brought the extraordinary gift of a fledgling hummingbird alighting on our deck. From what I could ascertain that first morning by witnessing this incredible sight, as well as information gathered from my books, it appeared this fledgling may have taken its first flight directly from the nest to our petunia-covered deck. I was standing near the kitchen window when I heard a soft, muffled peeping, unfamiliar to me. My eyes slowly scanned the length of the deck until they came to rest on a tiny hummingbird. He was sitting on the lip of a clam basket filled with petunias. He repeatedly peeped, and then shut his eyes, exhausted by his journey into a strange and unfamiliar place. His body was obviously that of a fledgling—fluffy, a bit chubby around the middle, not as sleek and streamlined as the adult, ruby-throated hummingbird.

I quietly stepped onto the deck, offering hushed peeps in return. To my amazement, the tiny bird sat firm, not at all concerned by my proximity. What did he have to fear? His life was still tender and free of the hazards that would come soon enough with the first few weeks of fledgling life. I sat close to him, talked in hushed tones, much as I used to do when volunteering at the Marin Wildlife Center in California. Back then, I was appointed to the bird room, a room crowded with broken wings and fragile newborns fallen from the nest, now resting in pint-sized incubators. I was assigned as caregiver to the naked newborns that, for whatever reason, would only accept sustenance from me, and if I softly spoke to them while gingerly fitting the tiny dropper into their beaks.

So, while I quietly spoke, the hummingbird appeared to become even more relaxed. Before I knew it, his peeping stopped, and his small body fell into what appeared to be a deep slumber. This only lasted a few moments and, with the sudden verve and energy that is a hummingbird, he flew upward and went headfirst into a petunia. After he enjoyed a long sip, he zipped alongside the planter boxes, dipping and fluttering as he drank the nectar from each new blossom. After filling his belly, again he alighted, but this time right in the middle of a deck plank. He peeped. I sat quietly nearby. He peeped again, louder. From somewhere in the depths of the pines not far from the deck, his mother flew in. While I sat only a couple of feet from them, she proceeded to feed her baby directly in front of me. I could not believe what I was seeing. From all I had read, very few have been given this incredible gift of seeing a mother hummingbird feeding a newly fledged bird outside of the nest! When she finished, she flew off but stayed close to the deck to keep a watchful eye on her baby.

I got nothing done that first day. But, if you look at it in other terms, I had experienced a once-in-a-lifetime adventure that was far richer than an armful of extraordinary happenings. I spent hours on the deck that afternoon. Around 4 o'clock, when John arrived home from work, I motioned him to come quietly to the deck. He joined my side, straining to see what I was pointing toward. Finally, his eyes rested on the fledgling hummingbird sitting on the lip of the clam basket, his new favorite perch. His eyes were closed, the warmth of the sun bathing his iridescent feathers, seeming to enjoy a daydream. Within a few moments, the baby awoke and began his peeping, a call he seemed to make to his mother when he needed reassurance, comfort, and additional sustenance. From around the side of the porch she flew, down to her fledgling once again, and this time for John's eyes. While we sat in awe, she regurgitated sustenance into her tiny baby's throat. Neither of us spoke, but we shared a silent moment of overwhelming emotion, and, when I looked at John's face, his eyes too were rimmed with tears. The sight of these two tiny and miraculous birds, mother and child, bonding was surely one of the most tender and beautiful sights we had ever witnessed.

Having been born in Maine, and like most true Mainers, this fledgling had a bad habit of waking at the crack of dawn. The following day, the first pink light of early morning barely on the horizon, I awoke to a constant peeping. This alarmed me: Was the fledgling in some sort of trouble? I jumped from bed and looked out our second-story window, scanning the deck, the potted plants, the clam basket. But I could not see him. The peeping continued, louder and close by. I hurriedly dressed and ran downstairs. I stepped onto the deck and listened. Peep. I looked over to a hanging, moss-covered basket that was attached to the shingles of the exterior wall. On the wire rim was the hummingbird. His tiny feet were curled around the scrollwork of the basket, his beautiful head pointed skyward. His eyes were closed, but he continued to peep. Was he peeping in his sleep? Or was he awake with his eyes closed? I peeped back, he answered, and I spent the rest of the morning sitting on the deck with a surrogate mother's mindful eye.

The first full week of his young life, I sat outside with him, chronicling his every new experience. I saw his first attempt at using the hanging nectar feeder and laughed aloud at what a feeble attempt it was. He had seen his mother use this feeder, but, when he flew to the rung, confused, he sat side-saddled, twisting his head sideways to use the feeder. Finally, after numerous attempts, he realized that he had to sit facing the feeding hole, not sideways. From his first day on the hanging feeder, I would talk to him and place my fingers next to the rung where he was sitting. He fed. After a few days, I would approach the feeder without the hummingbird, place my thumb and index finger on either side of the rung, and call him. Nearly every time, he flew up to the feeder, alighting between my fingers, his warm, tiny body brushing against my skin.

He spent most of his long, summer days on or near the deck, sleeping on a clay pot, on the side of the deck rail, in the moss-covered basket. I saw his mother feed him twice more that first week, and then he was on his own. Each afternoon, John would come home, bring a cold drink to the deck, and join on the watch. He would laugh when watching the hummingbird dip into a flower, its balance still awkward, his attempts at feeding clumsy and comical. Once, he got his head stuck too far down in the center of a large petunia, shook it out, and was on his way.

Subsequent days brought new aggression toward him from the adult hummingbirds. When the fledgling was at the hanging tube feeder, a dominant male would fly up to him and stab his little back with its sharp beak. The fledgling would quickly fly away to safer confines among the potted plants. Another time, an adult female showed aggression and so startled him that he flew into a kitchen window. Thankfully, he was unhurt. Naturally, this aggressive behavior toward the fledgling concerned me, but hummingbirds can be rather aggressive and all of this was a natural part of the learning process and hierarchy. By the end of his first week, the bird was gaining confidence and nerve, and did not always back down when bullied by an adult. This tiny bird was finding its way, determined to make the length of our deck and the bounty of blossoms his territory.

Three or four hummingbirds drank simultaneously at the hanging feeder on occasion. It was always easy to spot the young one, the only chubby body and a head sporting a buff hairdo. Although fledgling hummingbirds always have the coloring of an adult female, I believe this one was a male as he had two tiny, blackish feathers forming on his throat. By the following year, and if all went safely in his migration, he would have the lovely, iridescent-green throat that, when hit by sunlight, would appear a brilliant ruby red.

We spent the entire summer with this incredible creature. He felt as safe around us as he had with his mother. I do believe he enjoyed having his photo taken for John took over two rolls of film of him. From sleeping in the rugosa bushes, to alighting on a clay pot, to feeding from a blossom or the hanging tube feeder, his new life was recorded in stills. At times, while I sat in my Adirondack chair, gazing across the reach and cove, he would fly up to me and hover just inches from my face, his tiny, black eye looking into mine.

Those were extraordinary days. I watched him go from his first tender days, uncertain and insecure, to a thriving juvenile defending his territory. As the end of the summer approached, I knew the time was near when I would no longer see his familiar face. I dreaded that day yet knew it was inevitable, always hoping for a little more time. Then, one day, he was gone. No answer to my calls, no small body perched on the lip of a clay pot or basket. I remember swallowing hard the day I knew he was gone. I can only hope that he migrates safely to Central America, and that he has the wherewithal and energy to cross the vast waters of the Gulf of Mexico and back to his home in Maine, to our deck and to his bounty of petunias next spring.

CHAPTER 11

Carpe Diem

Tomorrow once again we sail the Ocean Sea.

~ Horace

John is becoming increasingly aware that his right leg and foot are now seriously compromised. The other night, before climbing into bed, he studied his calves. "The muscle is noticeably smaller on my right calf," he said, pointing to the spot where the muscle had started to collapse, causing an indentation running lengthwise. At first, I couldn't see it. Or was it that I didn't want to see it? After looking a second time, I could see that the muscle had, in fact, atrophied—not by much, but it was visible. We had been lucky thus far, his right hand being the only visible sign of atrophy, of inevitable paralysis. His legs, however, were a far more complex issue, and, in many ways, much more frightening than his hands. We had taken yet another step into the abyss.

Last weekend, we went to Bangor to see a movie. We stopped at the mall to look for a few things we needed and were walking along at a leisurely pace when John gently grabbed my arm and said, "Slow down, please." I wasn't walking faster than usual and, if anything, it felt like a relaxed stroll. Nevertheless, whatever the pace, it was too fast for John. His balance felt shaky, and he did not have the stamina to keep up. This caught me off guard as he had never before asked me to slow down, and I realized the effect on his right leg and foot was far more serious than I had thought. John is not a complainer. Far from it. And, while he has become increasingly honest and forthright about his fears and the progression of the disease, I must still initiate much of the conversation about how he is coping as he experiences the changes to and limitations of his body. "Your leg must frighten you. I know it scares me," I said later that night. When I had asked him this before, he had promised that he was fine with it, had accepted what was happening. But, this night, he admitted otherwise, and, as he wrapped himself around me, he whispered, "This is beginning to scare me, Jan." Dealing with his atrophied arm and hand had been one challenge, but now, seeing the disease move into his lower limbs, opens the door to a new set of problems, more complicated than ever before. This frightens me as well, even more than his left arm that is now showing signs of progression. His left hand is feeling weaker; the fasciculations are more frequent and profound. I worry about these "sudden" symptoms. It has taken a couple of years to adversely affect his right arm and hand; now, suddenly, his left hand is losing strength, and we are discussing a foot and ankle brace to better support his right leg. I am fearful that the disease is speeding up after a seemingly slow, prolonged progression. Many if not most ALS patients with limb onset die within two to five years upon receiving the diagnosis. Do we have less time than we've been hoping for? What will another year bring? Are we being unrealistic, foolish in thinking we can continue to dream—dreams about additional travel, life plans? We must continue to hope for the best, which can be done without being in denial or unrealistic. We must continue to plan for our future, for next year, for tomorrow. Otherwise, we will lose ourselves to this disease, becoming prisoners of its grisly prospects.

The next morning, I suggest we make an appointment with a specialist to get John fitted with a foot and ankle brace. His balance continues to be precarious, and it will only get worse.

He is tripping on a regular basis. His foot and toes drag, drop foot, catching on carpets and steps. John seems open to the idea but, as the days slip by, he seems less and less interested. I am not sure if it is in part denial or the fear of "giving in" to a prosthetic device. Either emotion, I can understand. While the signs of disease are obvious in John's arm, there is nothing that screams "disabled" or "handicapped" about his condition. Will relying on a prosthetic device make him feel this way? In his mind, crippled? I worry about his loss of balance, of him falling, becoming prematurely tired as he overcompensates for the weakness in his right leg. Many ALS patients succumb to head injuries sustained in falls. I will have to respect and rely on his better judgment. I do believe he knows of his limitations, and I don't think he will take foolish or unnecessary chances. But I'm still fearful, much of the time.

I try to remain optimistic, as does John, in dealing with this horrific disease. But, the other evening, and for the first time, he said something in passing that surprised me more than I would have liked. He had purchased a new pair of pants and was modeling them for me after dinner. "These are really great pants," he said, and I agreed. As he headed into another room, beneath his breath I heard him say, "If I thought I was going to live much longer, I'd buy another pair." He laughed, but his levity couldn't hide the seriousness of his words. It was the first time he had ever spoken of his impending death with any kind of timetable or urgency. "Don't say things like that," I smiled, giving him a long, hard embrace. "If you like these pants so much, buy another pair." "I know," he chuckled, but his words were a reminder that, no matter how hard we try to live day by day and as normally as possible, thoughts of impending death and dying are never far enough away.

Today, John brought home a shopping bag filled with books. Books on France, a world atlas, and miscellaneous maps. "France!" he smiles. John suffers from a case of wanderlust that equals my own. He is a seasoned traveler, much more than I, and during his early 20s lived in Europe for well over a year. He spent the greatest amount of time in Paris and Vienna, and island hopped in Greece. But it was France that stole his heart, and I was thrilled that my first trip there and subsequent trips as well have been with John as my partner and guide. And, as we no longer have the perceived luxury of time for putting things off, a return trip to France is on the top of the list before the progression of John's disease worsens.

We have found a few small belongings to sell to help finance the trip, allowing us the month of April to savor the French countryside and Paris. We agree on a tiny cottage in Provence for the first two weeks, in an area we know and love. We will rent in the small town of L'Isle-sur-la-Sorgue, a perfect jumping-off point for exploring the surrounding wine region. We will be steeped in art and history, enveloped by ancient, picturesque villages; sprawling vineyards; Roman ruins; cafés and bistros. Life is slower there, more relaxed. No one is in any great hurry. Meals are leisurely and enjoyed over hours of good conversation and wine.

April in Paris. Cherry trees in full bloom and bursting with color, horse chestnuts dripping with heavy blossoms. We will rent along the rue Cler, a favorite street. We know this stretch of pavement with its lively marketplace. We have our favorite bakery nearby, Poujauran, for its mouth-watering almond croissants and buttery pastries. Our favorite cheesemonger with his creamy brie and sharp morbier. The produce suppliers rim the street with their colorful masterpieces of fruits and vegetables, arranged in artful displays and impossible mounds.

After two lazy weeks in the countryside, we will be ready for the energy of the city: the museums, subway, and bistros bustling with activity. During the evenings, we will stroll the boulevards or tiny back streets and passages, enjoying the warmth of golden light in windows and cafés. We will walk along the Seine and admire the city lights glistening in its reflective waters. The air will be heavy with perfumed blossoms and dainty wrists. Our bodies will be warmed by each other and good wine. France in April is always good for a smile.

Yet these sweet sounds of the early season,
And these fair sights of its sunny days,
Are only sweet when we fondly listen,
And only fair when we fondly gaze.
There is no glory in star or blossom
Till looked upon by a loving eye;
There is no fragrance in April breezes
Till breathed with joy as they wander by.

~ William Cullen Bryant

CHAPTER 12

Migrations

Goodbye to All That.

~ Robert Ranke Graves

March, 1999

If our lives didn't already feel out of step with the rest of the world—and, at times, surreal—midweek compromised our balance yet again, as we found ourselves standing among images of gray and white and black, surrounded by gravestones. Our wonderful friend, Consi, had died. She was more than our friend; she was in the truest and deepest sense, family. It was through Consi's prodding and encouragement, her love of world travel that we ventured to Africa together, for the trip of a lifetime. It was to be her last, great adventure.

Our neighbor in Maine, Consi split her time between Sargentville and the suburbs of Atlanta. But Maine was her true love, and she longed for early summer when her bags were packed and she flew northward, like a migrating bird, to her familiar territory, her roost along the rugged shore. From the first time we met, we became instant friends; a bond created from an innate sense of ease and familiarity that is usually reserved for a handful of lifelong friendships, or amongst the warmth of family. Consi's friendship and unconditional love enriched our lives in ways that will forever be engrained in how we live the remainder of our days. Our friendship was kismet and, from the six and a half years we knew her, we will carry with us a lifetime of cherished memories.

As we stood in the middle of Atlanta's Oakland Cemetery, surrounded by tombstones of Consi's family members and those of the Civil War dead, I watched a gathering of crows fly low overhead, cawing noisily, circling directly above. Consi loved crows, as do John and I, and I couldn't help but feel that they were paying respect to another great bird. The wind howled in the near freezing daylight; an occasional snow flurry dropped from a slate sky. Only yesterday, it had been 75 degrees. But, today, Consi's day, it was blustery and frigid. So unlike the great lady who worshipped the sun, who wore only the colors of bright, tropical birds and showy blossoms, always a study of pinks and purples and island corals. The scene of black and gray and white did not reflect the life of Consi but reflected the sorrow and emptiness felt by those who loved her, the loss of a wonderful and free spirit.

As the days slip by, we have only begun to feel the extent of our loss. Consi had been our greatest support system in dealing with John's illness. When she was at home outside of Atlanta, rarely did a day go by that she didn't call to see how things were, to tell a good joke, to discuss food or travel. If she didn't call, we called her. She had suffered a small stroke not so long ago, and the near daily calls, for all of us, were to boost our spirits, make sure all was okay. She and John would share their fears, their like experiences. They talked of watching their bodies change, not having any control over what was happening to them, and what the future might hold. They gave each other pep talks and words of comfort, even if not always realistic. But honesty was always there too, as with any true friendship, and none of us ever withheld truths about the hands we had been dealt, no matter how difficult. From her easy chair in Georgia and across the phone lines to Maine, we would talk about her loss of freedom from the effects of her stroke, her hate for her walker, the myriad pills she had to swallow each day, her diabetes, and her determination to drive again. She'd ask about John's progressing symptoms, our impending trip to France, and about getting fit so she could return to her beloved home in Maine. She so looked forward to getting back to Bonnie Brae, her shingled cottage on the shore; in years gone by, she had confided in me that her hope was to die in Maine, in her pale purple bedroom overlooking the cove. It was not to be.

Part of Consi's ashes will be buried at Bonnie Brae next summer, as she requested, in the lavender Ball jar she kept separate from the others, all things purple, and within the sight and smell of the sea. We used to kid Consi about how we had erected 10 birdfeeders around our house and the money spent in feeding hundreds of birds each year, only to have them choose to nest at Bonnie Brae. Along its eaves, the surrounding branches, tucked in corners and porch rafters, all places within Consi's nurturing realm. She was the ultimate mother and friend. It only seems right that winged life and feather-light spirits should choose to have their families beneath the warmth and security of Consi's brightly colored wings.

Consi's death has been a particularly hard blow to John. I have seen him shed more tears in the last week than ever before. Somehow, she made him believe, made us believe, that all would be okay, if only for a short while. Her sudden death has also brought our own fears of mortality to the forefront, causing the flood of emotions to run rampant. Perhaps this is good, cathartic in some way. Our own hidden fears of death and dying, so near the surface, have now become exposed and raw.

Perhaps by releasing those fears into the light, it will allow a bit more room inside for hope and shared memories.

Last night I couldn't sleep. I thought of Consi, of John, about the progression of his illness, and what another year might bring. I realized that I could no longer "book" a dream so far in advance as our days of being assured of anything were slowly slipping away. What if John needs a cane in another year? What if he is confined to a wheelchair? What if his hands no longer work; his legs, what if? I tossed and turned out of fear and frustration until the early-morning spokes of sun fingered their way through the lace curtains. Now, John speaks of his left hand getting weaker. I must open "stubborn" jars and caps. He walks with a limp. His right arm hangs unnaturally; his hand caving in, looking disfigured. Is it sudden? It has taken a couple of years for his right arm to reach this stage of atrophy, of degeneration. But, in a matter of weeks, it has reached his left hand and right leg. It isn't only that his foot drops and rolls. He cannot get the correct movement, the mechanics of lifting his leg into motion. What will another year bring? Another month? Were we foolish to plan a month-long trip to France? What about all of the plans we've talked about: visiting his sister in India, my sister in the United Arab Emirates, experiencing the wildebeest migration in Kenya? What about anything?

Full daylight. My nightmares have left me exhausted and emotional. Last night, for what felt like the first time, although I am sure it was not, I realized that my life, our lives together, will never be the same. I am not ready for this realization. I needed more time to prepare—if such a thing exists. I must write to a dear friend in San Francisco, who lost her husband to AIDS just a few years back, and tell her of my fears. She will understand, as best as anyone can. I look at myself in the mirror, in that harsh and unforgiving morning light, and think I have aged a decade, overnight. I feel like an old woman trapped in a 40-year-old body. I feel as though I have lived and aged several lifetimes during the course of those long, dark hours. I tell my friend of my worries, my darkest fears, of feeling prematurely old and heavy with burden. Have I lost all youthfulness? All joy? Will I ever regain that lightness of spirit that I was so acutely aware of and took for granted for so many years?

Not an hour after my email, my friend's reply came across my screen. Her words of experience and wisdom helped me get through the day.

Jan: Thank you so much for your email. The phone call last weekend, and talking with you, did wonders for my soul too. I hung up feeling like my conversation with you and with John was the first conversation in what feels like forever that I talked about what is really important in life, what life is truly about. Your plans for France sound heavenly, and I understand your fears of it not happening. Hell, there are so many things that can happen between now and then that don't have a thing to do with John's health. Just life is all. Life and its unflinching determination to be bloody and utterly unpredictable. So don't worry, Jan. Go ahead and plan, plan for the best — and hopefully, you'll get lucky. I think the simple acts of planning and dreaming spark the heart. Lord knows, it helped us get through some really tough spots. And, as I recall, we were always able to eventually do everything we ever planned. It doesn't surprise me a bit that you feel old. You are older now than a lot of people your age — but in a good and beautiful way. I swear! I know it sounds woo-woo, and I'm almost embarrassed to write it, but there you go. It's true. You're wiser and more open, and it will show, no doubt. But I know you don't look ragged or like an old woman. It's really important to remember this. You will always be beautiful no matter what you go through. Because what you're going through is all about love, and one can't help but wear that well ...

CHAPTER 13

Provence and Paris

*Provence is not a country nor the home
of a race, but a frame of mind.*

~ Ford Madox Ford

After hours of jetlag, our first full day in Provence begins appropriately in the tiny village of Gigondas, a hamlet proud of and known for its full-bodied red wines. Hungry, and still exhausted, we settle in a bustling café—a perfect respite from the now steady rainfall. It's lunchtime, and naturally the café is crowded, smoky, and wonderfully French. The small, ubiquitous dog greets us at our table and nudges our legs, looking for a handout of salty ham or sugar cube. We order large salads of fresh greens and hard-boiled eggs, sweet tomatoes and briny olives, creamy omelets with a handful of fresh herbs. To initiate our arrival in our beloved Provence, we order a bottle of Raspail, one of Gigondas's celebrated wines. The cool breeze and occasional downpour calls for this rich, heady wine. While our first day may not offer the characteristic warmth of the Provençal sun, there is no doubt in our minds that we are miles from home, and chinking our glasses we exchange weary smiles and knowing looks, as if to say, "We made it!"

Next morning, the unrelenting mistral wind makes for a crystal-clear sky and penetrating sunshine. There is a unique clarity to the light in Provence, an intense, white light that stings the landscape. This razor-sharp focus illuminates with blinding clarity, the otherwise soft, hazy shapes of cypress and olive trees, rows of lavender and rosemary, and hills covered with blossoming cherry orchards making the contrast in color and texture, a favorite amongst artists and writers for centuries.

We drive toward Mont Ventoux, crossing the mountains toward Sault, the lavender capital of Provence. The mountain air is crisp and cool, thick with the refreshing smell of scrub pine and damp forest bramble. The drive is lovely, winding through chalky, terraced cliffs, and working downwards to miles of lavender fields not yet in bloom but warm and fragrant from the blazing sun. The landscape is complete with a maze of neat, clean rows of promising grapevines and a thousand cherry trees dripping with white snow-like blossoms. Perched on a hillside is the beautiful village of Sault where we enjoy a leisurely stroll through the town square, stopping at an aromatic patisserie for fresh apple turnovers, custard-filled pastries, and an egg-rich brioche.

The next day we rise early and head to Le Barroux and the Abbey Saint-Madeleine. We have been here before, for the spiritually penetrative chanting of the resident monks, and knew we would have to return someday. This morning—except for a single monk who sits at the organ, filling the tiny chapel with melancholy riffs that echo across the thick, stone walls— John and I sit alone. I close my eyes and secretly say another prayer for John, for remission of disease: "Please, God. Please slow it down. Please help us."

Tonight, we treat ourselves to a wonderful dining experience at the Mas de Cure Bourse, just outside our village. The dining room is part of an elegant, 18th-century farmhouse with high, beamed ceiling, massive fireplace, and linen-draped tables. We begin our feast with a 1994 Gigondas and order from the four-course, prix-fixe menu, which, at $30 per person, seems like an extraordinary value. We start with a delicate serving of pâté wrapped in a smoky bacon strip and served with a small mound of pickled red onions. John follows with a flaky and moist cod cake with a smooth aioli, a garlicky mayonnaise, and julienned vegetables. I opt for paper-thin slices of smoked salmon, smooth and buttery, and marinated in just a hint of lemon juice, topped with wedges of sweet grapefruit providing the perfect balance. We relax for a while between courses, enjoying the warmth of the blazing fire and candlelight. With perfect timing, our waiter serves our main courses: for John, steak stuffed with olive tapenade and a courgette (zucchini) blossom filled with chicken mousse; for me, a game bird roasted in port and herbs, surrounded by a creamy potato galette, and tender snow peas and baby carrots. We have little to say to one another. Food and wine are two of our passions, and I'm grateful that John's appetite has not yet waned due to his illness. Instead, rather, he is fixated on his plate, and his small grin speaks volumes. To cleanse our palettes after a much-needed interlude, our cheese course arrives with wedges of brie with tapenade and Roquefort with sliced pears.

Just when we think that it's not humanly possible to eat another bite, our stomachs surrender, and we indulge in a moist, coconut gateau, resting in a pool of chocolate sauce with a smattering of plump raspberries, and warm crème brûlée with tender, sweet figs. The proprietors must be masochists, and we give in without a struggle to a complimentary tray of tiny confections—dollops of meringue, miniature citron tarts, chocolate truffles, and squares of local nougat. We entice this down with a shared glass of the local dessert wine from Beaumes de Venise: smooth, floral, and aromatic.

After a three-hour dining marathon, John suggests we drive to the tiny medieval village of Sauman, perched on a hill. He wants to see the bath of full moonlight cast across the surrounding countryside. In the shadows of an empty and darkened town square, we hug each other tightly and look across the illuminated landscape. For a few moments, the heaviness of our lives is lifted, and, if only for a shared heartbeat, seems to dissipate into the silence of a moonlit evening.

We are returning today to the ancient town and chateau ruins of Les Baux, enclosed by miles of vines, olive groves, and the sculpted white cliffs of the Alpilles mountain range, a wall of rock that reminds me of a giant, prehistoric backbone. Somehow, and miraculously, John is able to make the steep, rough climb to the chateau tower. I am amazed that he has managed this climb, his leg weaker than ever before, his limp exaggerated. We've done very little walking. Sadly, most of our views have been from within our rental car. As so many of these ancient villages have uneven cobbled streets, John isn't comfortable with too much walking, fearing a trip or fall. His energy level is no longer the same as it used to be; he fatigues so much easier now, stops to catch his breath. Exploring this region on foot used to be one of our great joys. But now we drive slowly by, admiring what we can from behind car windows, as others snake their way on foot through tiny, secret passageways and ride bikes along roadsides dotted with wildflowers.

This trip has not been easy, and I'm having a very difficult time. I wanted to fully enjoy this holiday in France, but I'm finding the underlying issues of John's declining health to be overwhelming. Things are no longer subtle. He is perpetually tired. This frightens me. John, of anyone I've ever known, has always been blessed with unlimited energy. I try to set these fears aside, but they creep into my mind at night, making most sleep hours short and unrestful. His drop foot and limping, his lack of balance, are so much worse, more profound just since we have been here. I know I must try to live day by day, not to become devastated by the crippling effects that are beginning to take hold of John. But the emotional human psyche and my love and concern for him are causing me a great deal of angst. Is this our last trip here? Anywhere? How can I enjoy myself when I see the person I love most struggling with his hands, struggling to walk, to keep up? I'm exhausted from little sleep, and he sees this, of that I'm sure. He knows me; he knows I am not as happy as I would otherwise be in this glorious place. But how could I be? And, while he remains upbeat, I sense he feels the same. We are protecting each other with feigned happiness and optimism. But there is no doubt: Some of the sharp, clear light of Provence has lost its focus.

We are excited about our day trip to the Camargue, a vast and marshy wilderness of low-lying plains, noted for its white horses, black bulls, migrating birds, and French cowboys. The Camargue, located near the Mediterranean Sea, is home to the Parc Ornithologique, a 30-acre reserve that offers sanctuary to thousands of migratory birds from northern Europe and Siberia on their way southward to warmer climes. We have been here once before and were mesmerized by the scores of pink flamingos dancing through ponds and wetlands, the cages filled with majestic eagle-owls and other birds of prey. The Parc cares for and rehabilitates injured birds with the intent of release. However, if they cannot be released back into the wild, they are caged in large enclosures and cared for as educational birds for the visiting public.

The afternoon is lovely. While we revel in the graceful beauty of the nesting egrets, myriad hawks, eagles, and abundant waterfowl, something extraordinary occurs: a happening so fantastic and moving that it defies definition. And, for lack of a better description, and what some will surely call anthropomorphizing, I will refer to it as a "cross-species" communication, as I have never been a part.

I see an injured raven in a large enclosure filled with hawks. It's the only raven in the cage. It sits high within the enclosure, its body crouched on a perch. The Grand Corbeau, as it's called, sees me, is watching me. I can feel its eyes following me as I excitedly leave John's side and approach the cage. I make eye contact with the bird, followed by my best hoarse raven call. Instantly, the raven swoops down from its perch, landing on the ground behind the chain-link fence and directly in front of me. It's only inches from where I kneel. It quickly moves to the fence and sticks its beak toward me through an opening, tilting its glossy head so its eye is focused directly into mine. I offer another feeble attempt at a raven croak, and it answers, croaking back. There is something wrong with its voicebox, and its response is hoarse and quiet, more of a whisper. Nonetheless, it continues to cough out its raspy caws, all the while pushing its beak closer toward me.

John, now at my side, is captivated, as are others who have collected around us to watch this raven's extraordinary behavior. Suddenly, the bird begins to pull dried grass from the edge of the fencing, filling its beak and offering me mouthfuls of grasses. "Take them!" John says excitedly. I gently pull the grasses from its beak and set them in a neat pile on the opposite side of the fence. I offer a tiny twig in return, which the raven accepts and places on its side of our barrier.

Again, it offers materials. Nesting materials, I wonder? It continues to pull grass and twigs from the earth's floor, all of which I accept. This time, I find another twig and, through the small opening of the linked fence, I begin to allopreen the raven, gently stroking and combing beneath its throat, along the back of its head. This is a common ritual among corvids, and the raven appears to be enjoying it, closing its eyes as I stroke it, all the while offering each other hushed caws and croaks.

Stones, now. The raven spots a smooth stone and lifts it into its beak. It sets the stone at the edge of the fence and pushes it through. Pebbles, another stone. It starts a pile of "nesting materials" in front of me: more dried grasses, evergreen twigs. A small mound is forming, neat and contrived. John snaps photos of the raven's extraordinary actions as a handful of adults and many children move even closer, silently watching. Again, the raven pushes its body into the fence, and, although I shouldn't, I cannot resist touching this amazing bird. At first, I feel a bit apprehensive; its beak is sharp and powerful. "Go ahead!" John coaxes. "It wants you to ..." I touch the top of its head with my fingertips, smooth and warm. I stroke the back of its neck and beneath its chin. I feel the silkiness of its glossy feathers. I see its eyes upon me. At this moment, I am unaware of anything around me except for the attention of this raven, the connection between animal and man. It was as if the raven knew how I felt, my profound love and respect for all animals. Whatever this was, it was an intense, magical, and unique moment. It was a shared bonding. It only reaffirms my belief that we should respect all creatures, and the indisputable connection between all living things.

Ravens are said to be one of the most intelligent of bird species. This particular raven seemed to thrive on my attention, my awkward attempt at communication. It appeared to need stimulation, a connection, and I offered this great bird a singular moment unto itself, personal and heartfelt. I have read many accounts of the raven's intelligence. But, after today's remarkable experience, there is no doubt of the incredible mind of the raven, however sad or poignant, in going through the motions of a nesting bird, offering materials, and accepting mine. I would like to think that, if only briefly, I offered this raven something out of the ordinary, a moment freed from its caged prison—if only in its mind—and in deep gratitude for the wonderful memories it gave to me.

Reluctantly, we leave Provence. But, with great anticipation, we board the high-speed train for Paris. From the Gare de Lyon, we hail a cab and head to our rental apartment on the Passage rue Nicot in the 7th arrondissement, on the Left Bank. We lug our bags up two flights of steep, narrow steps to our tiny studio apartment. John is barely able to climb the two flights and, every few steps, he must stop to rest. Reaching the top, he is badly flushed and out of breath.

Just a block away is our favorite street, rue Cler. Along its colorful path we find a wonderful cheesemonger or fromager, and stop for a sharp morbier and creamy camembert. Off to the chicken rotisserie, then wines and pastries. We save our last stop for the sumptuous delights at patisserie/boulangerie Poujauran, just down the street from our studio, and marvel at the decadent pastries, the olive and nut-plumped breads and rolls. With our feast bundled in our arms, we move toward home, but not before John rips off a mouthful of baguette, still warm, crunchy, and tender.

After yesterday's long travel hours, we get a late start and opt for exploration near our apartment. We stroll to the Rodin museum, one of our favorites, and, after a quick walk through, we stop to rest in the lovely gardens overflowing with pale lilacs and a profusion of colorful tulips. John is fatigued and, although we have done little walking, it is taking a toll on his energy. By late afternoon, we head back to the apartment. John is limping rather badly, his posture hunched over as if he can barely hold himself upright. He is short-tempered with cars and taxis that barely stop, hardly allowing us enough time to move through the crosswalks. Jokingly, he shakes his fist and shouts, "I'm walkin' here! I'm walkin' here!" as the vehicles screech to a halt for our crossing. He is mimicking the scene from the film *Midnight Cowboy* where the crippled Dustin Hoffman screams these words as he is nearly run down at an intersection. John laughs, easily. But, from the look in his eyes, I sense there is no real humor in his actions.

Tonight we dine at a neighborhood bistro, Thonieaux. It is a classic French bistro, bustling and full of life. The interior is subdued: maroon banquettes; small, dark wood tables; mirror-lined walls and soft golden lighting, which balances nicely with the otherwise manic energy of the wait staff. We start with fresh, local asparagus, followed by steamy crocks of cassoulet. The cassoulet is filled with moist and flavorful white beans, pungent garlic, tender duck, and a bit of salty ham. We share a split of Burgundy, which is the perfect complement to the meal. For dessert, white porcelain bowls overflowing with plump strawberries and crème fraîche, and poire au vin — a succulent pear stewed in red wine with vanilla bean ice cream.

The meal is fantastic, and we feel well fed and satiated. Just as we lean back to relax, John breaks into one of his drenching sweats. They seem to come out of nowhere and always catch him off guard. Suddenly, his face is burning scarlet and beads of sweat form across his forehead and upper lip, dripping down the sides of his face. His white shirt clings to his chest, damp. He loosens his collar and takes a few deep breaths, a sip of cold water. There is nothing we can do when he breaks into one of these sweats — a symptom that has baffled our doctor in Boston, a specialist in ALS. While they only last a few minutes, they seem to take a great toll on John, and he is left feeling wasted and out of sorts. Fortunately, this one passes quickly. We pay the bill and step outdoors into the crisp night air. Outside, on a quiet side street, we clench each other's waist and gaze up at the jewel of Paris before us, the sparkling lights of the Eiffel Tower gleaming against the cobalt evening sky. Slowly, we move toward the beacon, home.

Feeling rested this morning, John suggests a day at the Louvre. We spend most of the afternoon in the sculpture salons, mesmerized by the French, Greek, and Roman pieces. The Three Graces is a masterpiece, and we go back to it time and time again. Our pace is no longer what it used to be, and we cannot contend with the mad, fast-moving throngs of people rushing in and out of salons. We choose, today, to view only a small portion of the museum, focusing on and enjoying a tiny, savory bite instead of fast gulps and semidigestion of all that it houses. We can sit for hours in just a few salons, moving from seat to seat, feasting on a few select pieces. Slowing down for John's lack of stamina is a blessing, really. Masterpieces should not be rushed through or seen only through shoving elbows and over strange shoulders. They should be savored. So, if we can only see a small portion of the treasures of the Louvre, at least we are absorbing and appreciating even the minutest detail of a few precious works of art. And this suits us just fine.

Shopping day. We are in and out of Paris's great department stores — La Samaritaine, Galeries Layfette, Au Printemps, in search of warmer sweaters for an unseasonably cold April climate. Then, onto the gourmet food store, Fauchon, in search of black gold, truffles. John's leg and balance have been frighteningly worse today — each day has taken a bit more, and I am increasingly worried. He's tripped numerous times. His foot and toes are dragging, catching on department store carpets, cracks in the pavement. I am nervous he will fall. When we get home, he tells me, he will apply for a handicapped placard for our car. Another step in a direction I do not want to head.

We take a taxi back into our neighborhood and shop for our evening meal: another roast chicken, honey clementines, ripe tomatoes with fresh buffalo mozzarella, baguette from Poujauran's. It's damp and cold, and we are tired. Evenings have been dropping to freezing or below. We are happy to spend the evening in our warm, little apartment, with comforting food, smooth wine, and each other. Our energy reserves are spent throughout the course of our days and leave us little desire to revel in the Paris nightlife.

We spend the next day at the Musée d'Orsay admiring the French Impressionist paintings. Later and back in our familiar haunts, we slip into a café tabac, dodging a cold, pelting rain. We relax at a small table with café cremes, and John buys his daily cigar and newspaper. The café is crowded with small, wet dogs, which seem to outnumber the patrons. We enjoy their company and, only in France, can a tiny café filled with damp dogs be undeniably welcoming and utterly charming.

While the rain catches its breath, we rush back into the streets to gather our supper, olive-and-nut baguettes to accompany truffle omelets, a fresh melon for dessert. Poujauran's baking is nothing short of remarkable. We were overjoyed to find an apartment so close to his winsome boulangerie; it is a mystery how his croissants, baguettes, and pastries can be even more delicious than other masters of the art. His rolls are ethereal, stuffed with olives and hazelnuts, moist figs, flaky and buttery crusts. Admittedly, we have become Poujauran groupies and have no qualms about waiting in long lines for the masterpieces from his oven.

Each morning, John walks the half block to the bakery to buy our breakfast treats. They are beginning to know him there. He looks forward to the morning stroll, choosing the most delectable-looking pastries for our morning coffee. They know him there too because he has been dropping his change. Each time he goes to pay, the change does not sit flush across the palm of his atrophied hand. It rolls off, clanging across the counter or, worse yet, spilling onto the floor. There is always a line of people waiting at Poujauran's, and John's increasing inability to handle change or small objects takes him a bit more time in line. Just this morning, as he fumbled for correct change, it flew from his hand and rolled across the floor of the bakery. Carefully, because of his lack of balance, he crouched down to collect the money. After gathering it up, he rose, only to slam his head on the underside of a marble pastry table. The owner himself was standing behind the counter, and, as John reported, cringed at the sight of John's head slamming into the marble top, offering a fast smattering of French as to John's well-being. "I am okay," John pronounced in his semi-French, rubbing his head. "I am okay, but your table, sir ...." Poujauran grinned, nodded, and presented John a bag filled with warm pastries, which somehow eased the sting from the top of his head.

Next afternoon after a seafood lunch in the Marais, we walk to the Musée de l'histoire de Paris. It is a relatively small museum and houses lovely salons of 17th-century furnishings and artifacts chronicling the history of the city. We are not in best form today. Tired, I suppose. Perhaps the nonstop stimulation of three weeks of travel is taking its toll. We spend hours in the museum. With little or no seating in the salons, energy and stamina are fading fast. But John keeps pushing on. We have been here before, yet he is studying each piece as if it was his first time. He is moving slowly, hunched over, seemingly dragging himself from room to room. I say it is time to go, he looks very tired, but he is not ready. As the hours slip by, his color fades. For the first time, he looks ill, as though he is pushing himself too hard, ready to collapse. He is studying everything he sees, touching things he should not be touching. I see desperation in his moves; his almost frantic need to add tactile experiences to his visual ones. It is the desperation of a dying man. Again, I plead to leave. But, with sad resignation in his eyes, he says, "I want to see it all. This will be my last trip to Paris." His words are crushing. They hang in midair. My heart feels thick and bloated within my chest. I must compose myself although I am ready to weep. The way he looks, the finality of his words, are overwhelming. I walk from the salon and into another, searching for a room to myself. I am holding back a torrent of emotion; I must keep moving, people are around, and I do not want to cry—not in front of these strangers. Not that they matter really; it's just that I'm afraid I will not be able to stop.

I suppose I have known all along that this may be John's final trip here, our last trip together. Paris is his favorite city in the world. Hearing the quiet, resigned desperation in his voice, seeing him drag a body slowly losing strength and vitality from room to room, are reminders of the horrors this vacation was supposed to blur, diffuse. Maybe we were attempting to outrun reality on this trip. But there is nowhere to escape, nowhere to hide. It has finally caught up with us.

CHAPTER 14

A Season of Change

*... The grass must bend when
the wind blows across it.*

~ Confucius

We have been home for two months, and they have been the most difficult yet. A rapid series of losses and adjustments have left little time for pleasure, little time to collect our breaths. The reality of our lives has given a somber atmosphere to our days, and we have been negligent in finding some sort of outlet to help balance this emotional load.

While John tries to remain upbeat, even his gallant attempts at levity are beginning to falter or ring false. I struggle in using the term "handicapped," but his figure and demeanor no longer appear healthy or vibrant. There is something noticeably wrong. His limp continues to worsen, and he is now reliant on a cane. His left hand is failing, following suit with his right. The right arm has gotten extremely thin, his hand atrophying to what medical experts call the "swan hand"—the wasting of muscle, forcing the hand into a permanent curved or swan-like position. With both hands slipping away, it is only a matter of time before the cane is no longer manageable. He is tripping over things, rugs, thresholds, steps, falling on occasion, at times taking me down with him. I can move some obstacles from his path, but others are permanent and out of my control. He has lost a considerable amount of weight due to muscle atrophy as muscle weighs more than fat. There are moments when his speech is affected, and, although not often, it's quite obvious to us and a few others as well. When he is tired, his speech is thick and slurred; his voice softer, barely audible. This reality is perhaps the most frightening yet: The thought of the muscles that affect his speech becoming compromised is terrifying to both of us. Can the atrophying of the muscles used for swallowing be far behind?

Memorial Day. I sit on the deck watching osprey, a lone bald eagle, loons, and mother ducks with their ducklings swimming nearby, all thriving above and along the cove. The view is lovely. The color of June, purple, has come early, and the end of May offers lilacs and irises and the rise and fall of lupine giving way to the sea. Nestlings cry from their warm beds of twigs and feathers; hummingbirds vie for dominance along the flower-strewn deck. Everything appears normal. Life moves on with an occasional interruption, then settles back into the rhythm of procreation and existence. Time and life do not stand still for someone who is dying or has died. It keeps marching on to the beat of a dance created long, long ago. There are moments when I expect the world to come to a standstill, if only for a moment, in respect for the fate that has been bestowed upon John. But it will not. There will be those who suffer, who mourn. But each new day will bring healing in heart and spirit, in spring buds, newborns, the ebb and flow of tides, a magical harvest moon. Maybe it's that very normalcy of life, the familiar tugging of that rhythm and beat, that makes the loss of a loved one bearable. Perhaps if the world did come to a halt, and the Earth stopped revolving for a moment of silent respect, just perhaps that inconsistency of life — that sudden jolt — would knock one so off balance that getting to one's feet would be unattainable.

Another wake-up call. Yesterday, John's foot caught on a clump of grass and, before I could move to help, he spilled face down across the porch steps. It all happened so quickly. It was as if watching him fall in slow motion, his arms crumpling beneath him, his face slamming down against a step, the top of his head ramming hard into another. I could hear myself yelling, "No!" unsure of whether his head had split open or if he was even conscious. With much effort, I helped him to his feet and, to my horror, blood spilled from his mouth. I was profoundly relieved when I took a closer look. His top lip was split open; the inside of his lips were cut too. No teeth were missing or knocked loose, and, more important, the cuts did not appear to need stitching. His head was scraped raw, but, other than that, he had faired much better than we would have imagined. Inside, we tapered the swelling with bags of ice and caught our collective breaths.

The fall shook me up rather badly. John didn't seem quite as frightened as I, but it made him realize that the need for a foot and ankle brace was now imperative. I watched him closely throughout the evening. Did his head hurt? Any feelings of nausea? I worried that he may suffer from a slight concussion, but he slept soundly through the night and seemed okay the following day. The next morning, however, revealed a tremendously swollen and scabbed lip, a bruised and sore scalp. Before his coffee, he called a specialist in town recommended for fitting patients with orthopedic devices to aid in safety and comfort. Such a device will help to lift his foot and toes, which in turn should make tripping less frequent. He will also explore the possibility of using a splint-like device for his right hand. The use of a cane is no longer enough, or safe. We cannot take any more chances with his decreasing lack of mobility. The use of a walker is now imminent.

I am increasingly protective of John each day, as if I were looking out for the welfare of a child. Though he is not a child and still quite capable, I find that I must constantly be aware of his every move, always watching, processing, and anticipating. I will not always be there if and when he falls again. And this realization frightens me as much as anything. He no longer has the strength of his arms to brace himself during a fall. I just want to protect him, hold him, make sure he will be okay. I cannot bear the thought of anything else happening to him. But, in reality, this is only the beginning of things to come.

This morning I stretched out on the chaise lounge, enveloped in sun and colorful blossoms, and closed my eyes. I smelled the floral sweetness of the air mixing with the occasional briny scent of low tide rising from the shore. The birdfeeders were busy with parents and fledglings. Young crows barked their hoarse cries from somewhere in the stand of pines. I thought of happier times, of easier times. I thought of picnics, hikes to secret places where nesting osprey overlooked the warm sand beaches. I remembered our past vacations, hiking to a cabin in the Tahoe National Forest, high in the Sierra mountains, or the rental house along the rugged Mendocino coastline where we'd explore the lupine-filled meadows or collect driftwood along the crashing surf. I thought of the carefree days, walking cobbled streets in

Europe, the life-affirming adventures in South Africa. We cannot go to these places anymore, near or far. There are many places we can no longer go, John and I; many streets we can no longer stroll. Our lives were so much easier then, not so long ago. But, this morning, the sun is comforting, still. It feels like a warm blanket on my skin. Yet even beneath this warm blanket, I shiver at the loss of options and life choices once so commonplace and taken for granted, now seemingly drifting out to sea, and out of sight.

The late-summer sun hangs lower in the sky. The petunias are getting leggy and losing their leaves. In a matter of weeks, the hummingbirds will begin yet another migration southward to their winter homes. The osprey too will vanish from the September sky. Hummingbirds and osprey are harbingers of summer. And, while at first they announce promising days ahead, at last they remind us of a season coming to a close. When they are gone, the days and nights will turn chilly, longer nights will stretch into leafless mornings, and frost will not be far behind. Where did it go, the last year? It slipped away like sand; a rushed, grainy vision.

My family has come and gone. It was the first reunion in many, many years. My mother, my sister and her husband, my brother and his wife and their young daughters, all collected here to offer their love and support. It was bittersweet. I don't know if any of them will ever see John again. My brother's little girls, Shauna and Jessica, saw the ocean for the first time. They collected pocketfuls of rocks and shells, and neatly tucked them into their luggage. They pranced around John like tiny gazelles, giggling at his every word. They followed him, small shadows, determined to see his every move. They called him Crazy Uncle John because he made them laugh, made them feel special. Two things that he does best.

Next week, good friends from San Francisco arrive. For some of them, it will be seven years since they have seen John. They are here at my request, to celebrate John's 50th birthday. Graciously, and with open hearts, they accepted my invitation to visit Maine, to surprise John on the occasion of his birth. They juggled work schedules and small children to make this trip, and I am forever grateful. A few other close friends could not make it—money issues, or too busy, they said. They haven't seen John for some time and, more than likely, never will again. This makes my heart sink. Nevertheless, most are rising to the occasion. It's an eye-opener, terminal illness. Many friends become strong shoulders of support and offer unconditional love; others cannot face the inevitable, the hand we've been dealt. But, sadly, if and when these few come to terms or acceptance of their friend who is dying, it may be too late.

As the months have passed by and John's condition worsened, many friends and neighbors have stepped forward to offer their support. It lifts my spirit and lightens my heart to see these people come through for us. Their gestures of care have been a comfort to both John and me. Many times after a phone call from a distant friend or acquaintance, I can detect tears in John's eyes. "That was so nice of him to call," he'll smile. "I'm really touched by their concern." He knows he is loved. What more can one hope for in life than to be good, to love, and to be loved?

133

As a few friends back away, unwilling or unable to deal with difficult life issues, newer friends who once hovered on the periphery make gallant efforts to step within the circle. We want to help, they say. We want to do whatever we can. I cannot tell these people how important their words are, their heartfelt gestures and deeply felt compassion. Again, as our eyes are opened wider to the human condition, some of those we thought of as good friends may blur from our vision, while others we hardly know are moving closer, becoming all the clearer.

With the exception of a few close friends from the Bay Area, it is still rare for anyone here to inquire as to how I'm fairing. This continues to baffle me. Do they not know of my suffering too? Why don't they understand the pain involved in watching a loved one slowly dying, slipping away? Can they not empathize, even remotely, with what it means to have your entire life ripped apart, to realize that a future with your beloved does not exist, that part of me is dying as well, as I prepare for the death of my partner, the greatest love of my life? As most young couples do, we had planned on a lifetime together. We had hopes and dreams like everyone else. We knew, as a pair, we could embrace life as never before; grow old with one another; look outward, together. We shared a compassion and concern for all life, for nature, a common bond that wove its way tighter and tighter as the years slipped by. Each year has brought us closer together and more in love. I am a part of John, and he a part of me.

How can anyone not understand the gravity, the loss of purpose and being that I struggle with every day as I anticipate my life without John? As I watch him struggle and unhappy. As I watch him fall, again and again, spraining a knee, injuring an elbow, bruising a shoulder. As I see his breathing become labored, his body shutting down. As I massage each night his once strong hands, now slack and weak. As I hear his lovely voice becoming thick and slurred more than ever before. Can anyone fully understand the palpable pain of heart and spirit as your greatest love says he does not want to be a burden? That, as he continues to lose mobility, the loss of his legs, he sees himself only as a burden to me, ruining my life? They are crushing blows, these words. Paralyzing. How many times can I tell him that he will never be a burden to me? That I would gratefully take him, love him, in any way, shape, or form, as opposed to not having him in my life. The idea of life without him is devastating. His pain, in seeing himself as a burden, unbearable. I tell him that, before him, I did not know what love was, and I cannot expect to find such love again. He opened my heart. He made it blossom and soar. Maybe it's best that most people cannot fully understand. It is a pain far too excruciating to bear, even for one only peering in — from the outside.

Another aspect of dealing with terminal illness is the need to take care of oneself. I have always been good at taking care of others, but it's imperative that I now look out for my own well-being. I am good to no one, especially John, if I am not strong of body and mind. This is hard at times. Nearly 24 hours a day, I live for John, through John and his illness and his varied needs. This leaves little time for me. I must be true to my needs, however, respect what feels right for both of us, at any given moment.

As is John's nature, most days he'd prefer to be socializing, even with his decreased energy. But all of his needs are being taken care of, by me, which leaves me spent and with little reserve, emotionally or physically. I need to find a balance, somehow, of not only taking care of John, planning social activities here, dinner parties, running the household, but for what will also replenish my spirit—quiet time, reflection, time to cope, alone, and ultimately coming to terms with our fate. This balance is often difficult for couples dealing with death and dying. The ill partner, John, at times looks outward, needing the stimulation of and interaction with close friends and family as their days become numbered. The caretaker, me, often exhausted, of both mind and body, longs for time and glimpses inward, introspection, and an attempt to make sense of an otherwise nonsensical universe. Over the years, John and I have perfected what works best for us, together and separately. We respect one another's needs. This is important. I have always been comfortable with time alone. But, sooner than I would have liked, I will have no choice in the matter. Being alone and lonely are two very different animals, and I don't pretend to know what my life alone will be like. Alone with the constant, deafening silence. My life without John.

John is unsure as to whether or not he will choose to be in a wheelchair. It is one thing to be wheelchair-bound with an unlimited future; it is another to be in a chair, facing terminal illness. When he confessed this to me, I couldn't speak. Tears washed down my face and neck. I could not move. All along, we had discussed his being in a wheelchair, that we would adapt the house, and that I knew I'd be able to care for him. This was never my biggest fear, and yet, all along, it was John's. Early on, when post-polio appeared to be his fate, he had thought that he could bear the loss of his mobility, the loss of his legs. But not now.

"But how can the loss of your legs represent all that is precious and good in your life?" I wept. "How could that diminish your love of music, of laughter, family and friends, of good food and wine, fledgling hummingbirds, soaring bald eagles?" I pleaded. But he reminded me, as he gently touched my hand, that when his legs go, more than likely other symptoms will be taking their toll as well — his voice, his ability to swallow, to breathe. He has never wanted to "live" with a breathing ventilator or a feeding tube. This, I understand and respect. These are his wishes; his choices. But, not so secretly, I had hoped — perhaps selfishly — that being confined to a wheelchair was something he could live with, could tolerate. That his senses would compensate for the loss of movement, and that perhaps his beloved Bach cello or Mozart's strings would play like never before, an autumnal sunset would take on biblical bursts of color, and that my profound and undying love could sustain him. But we who don't contend with such darkness can ever presume to know, to fully understand what any of this means.

Ultimately, it is John's decision, and his alone. I cannot attempt to convince him otherwise for my own selfish reasons; to choose only to live because I love him, because I don't want to lose him. What I do want, however, is his happiness. And, when he no longer feels it, when each day becomes more of a burden than a blessing, then I must find the strength to let him go. To let go, out of love. And, somehow, I will let go, for John's sake. I will find the strength from those blackened depths that most of us hope never to pull from.

In the meantime, John has promised to give it more thought. He cannot promise me anything, but he will perhaps give the chair a try, but only if the rest of him is functioning and living on a somewhat normal basis, especially if he can still eat and swallow without choking, and his breathing is not compromised. He is not someone who gives up easily, but he does believe in quality of life. He is a fighter. He is a lover of life. He is the happiest human being I have ever known. He has learned and perfected how to live each day to its fullest, long before the disease took hold. He has had, he smiles, an incredible life. These words he offers to me. A gift. A precious gift.

I would not trade a single day with John, even with all the hardships and heartbreak, the struggles we've encountered and those yet to come. Our lives together have been too good, extraordinary, and a lesson in love. We have experienced more living and loving in the few short years we've had together than most couples do in a lifetime. We found each other, and that was the greatest gift either of us could have wished for. No regrets.

I stroke his head, his face. I pull my fingers, softly, across his eyelids, his lips, outline his nose. I feel the softness of his earlobes, push my fingers through his beautiful hair. His are the bluest eyes I have ever seen. I rub his neck, run my fingers down his shoulders. He smiles. His skin is warm and fragrant. I curl around him, enveloping his body with mine. I take a bit longer to touch him; I linger over the scent of his hair, his neck, the fullness of his lips. I do not want to forget these things. How he feels, the smell of his skin. Uniquely his. I do not want to forget. My soft strokes to his handsome face have relaxed him, and he drifts to sleep. I join him there.

The morning is beautiful. The sky, endless. Clear blue and refreshing winds. I hear the crows screaming and see the lovely, resident fox running through the meadow. The soft sunlight filters into the house and spills across tabletops as the lace curtains billow from the windows. This is a happy home, still. It is the home we chose for ourselves, our new life in Maine, nearly seven years ago now. It is a place we have filled with love and life, friends and family, and there is room enough for more. We have memories here, to be cherished. Against the mounting odds, we will find new ways to cope, to balance what is yet to come.

John is out sailing today. Sailing the lovely waters of the reach and bay. His great friend, Dave, maneuvers John onto his boat, picking him up if necessary. He will feel the wind on his back, the sun across his face. He will feel the salt spray against his skin, will rejoice at the sight of seals and osprey. He will come home energized and full of life. He will tell me of all he has seen, the life above and beneath the waters. We will sit on the deck come early evening, enjoying a cool drink as we revel in the bounty that surrounds us. If lucky, we will see the mother porcupine and her baby, the young buck, the doe with her fawns, the two mother raccoons with their four cubs, a broad-winged hawk, and, always, hummingbirds. Sailboats and schooners will tick across the reach, loons will cry out from the cove. And then there will be the goldfinches. Tiny parakeets. They are nesting now, forming bonds. They will chase one another and sing their melodic love songs. They will fly skyward, in a dance of sorts, two tiny male bodies fluttering against one another, vying for a female's attention.

Today was a good day.

PART II

Fade to Black

*Tell your heart that the fear of suffering is worse
than the suffering itself. And no heart has ever
suffered when it goes in search of its dream.*

~ Paulo Coelho

.

CHAPTER 15

A Day in the Life

*We are healed of suffering only by
experiencing it to the full.*

~ Proust

For the last year and a half or more of John's life, he was a quadriplegic. At the beginning of that time, he retained some mobility in his left hand, although limited. In time, the hand quickly slackened as the last of its muscles atrophied, and it joined the majority of his body, his muscles, which had previously wasted and lay paralyzed. The loss of that hand was heartbreaking as it robbed the last semblance of independence that John held onto, however minute it was. As long as he could slip a few crippled fingers through the handle of a baby cup and somehow lift it and its straw to his lips, he was doing something for himself. Psychologically, this was very significant. Now, there was nothing left he could do for himself even though, at that point, he was already reliant on all aspects of survival.

Each morning was much the same with a few variations along the way. I would wake relatively early after very little sleep, get dressed, and, if John still slept, would have my coffee and breakfast, allowing myself a few moments of downtime before the full-time caring for John began. When he woke, the first task of the day was to help him urinate, using the plastic bottle purchased at the medical supply store. Getting him dressed and out of bed were challenging. With time and practice it became somewhat easier. But, as his pain increased and his body deteriorated, it was a delicate operation not to hurt him in any way. First, I would dress him. Thick socks always, as his feet were perpetually cold, even on the hottest of days. Soft, fleece sweatpants were a staple; loose, elastic waist for comfort and cut open at the seams along the crotch so I could quickly and easily guide the urination process from his wheelchair. I would maneuver each foot into the leg of the pant, then, rolling John from side to side, work the pants up and around his hips and waist. T-shirts or sweatshirts were more difficult, as pulling each fragile arm into or out of a sleeve had to be done with great care so not to injure his wasted limbs, snap or fracture a bone.

Once he was dressed, I would pull the large, mechanical lifting device — the Hoyer lift — to the hospital bed that we had rented. No matter how many times I did this, and I did it at least twice a day for nearly two years, it was one of the most precarious operations. With John flat on his back, as he always was in bed, I would adjust the cradle-like, fabric sling beneath his hips, crisscrossing the flaps under and over his thighs. Each end of the "sling" was then attached onto the large, metal hooks and arms of the lift. I would sit him upright, holding him with one arm as I swung the Hoyer lift in front of him; then, manually with the other hand, hoist him up with the lift bar, swinging over the bed, airborne. While he was safe in this position, I would move his wheelchair into place, centered beneath John and the lift; then, very slowly, while directing his body with one hand, releasing the lift bar with the other, lower him, hopefully centered, into the seat of his wheelchair. Most of the time we got it right, but the lift was a heavy and awkward contraption, and it was critical to center John and very gently, as getting his body into the seat off kilter would cause him great pain. Once seated, I would remove the basket-like sling wrapped around him, release the Hoyer lift, and wheel him out of the leg grips of the lift. Just getting John out of bed at this stage was exhausting for both of us, particularly him. By the time he was positioned in his wheelchair, his face was often pale and haggard, and I could tell he was in some discomfort or pain.

Administering his medication was next. A low dose of oxycontin, just to take the edge off. Although his doctors thought he should be on a higher dose, John chose to "feel" the last days and months of his life. Two swigs of a prescription stool softener followed the pain meds, as the Catch-22 of pain medication is oftentimes extremely painful constipation from which John suffered greatly, body paralysis only worsening an already bad situation. I would brush his hair, usually pulling his long waves, now grown halfway down his back, into a ponytail; brush his teeth; wash his face.

I would wheel him into the kitchen for breakfast, or in front of the TV to watch a bit of the news, while I prepared soft toast or oatmeal, easier to swallow, and coffee or tea. I would feed him the toast, small bites, and slowly, as choking was a very real concern. The muscles used for swallowing atrophy, and many ALS patients die from choking. He choked on numerous occasions, but fortunately never to the point where his life was threatened, although he gave us a good scare more times than I would have liked. I would hold his cup as he sipped coffee or tea through a straw; a handful of vitamins, one by one, from vitamin E to alpha-lipoic acid to CoQ10—all supplements that were suggested as the result of ALS research.

When he was done with breakfast, John would either watch television or I would set him up with a book on tape. If he was particularly fatigued, he would ask to be positioned in front of the large, sliding-glass doors facing the cove and reach, and he simply observed. The songbirds, eagles, osprey, the waves and tides, cloud formations, all offered some form of comfort and peace of mind during those difficult days.

In the last year and a half, John left our home only three times. As we could not afford a wheelchair-accessible van, leaving home was no longer an option. Once, as he sat gazing out across the reach, I asked him if he missed anything, the rest of the world, if he felt trapped and contained. He smiled at me and said, "I have everything I need right here." And he meant it.

It was a continually amazing process to watch and experience the overwhelming acceptance and resilience of a dying man; the gradual adaptation to a changing and paralyzed body, to a different, foreign, and often frightening world. He accepted his limitations, embraced the true meaning of living and self-worth in ways that those living in a universe of mobility and good health cannot always grasp or ascertain. But, in many ways, this was not new to John. He, unlike anyone I had ever known, or have known since, had an innate sense of his place in the world, from early on. He lived life to its fullest, rarely wasted a day. He was perennially happy and upbeat, optimistic throughout the most trying moments. Because of this, and even before his illness, he was of constant amazement to others — most of all, me. As he would often say, it was not the quantity of life one lived but the quality. And, better than anyone, he knew this to be true.

We always found it a little perplexing though when we would hear or read accounts, often from a healthy bystander, that everyone suffering under the umbrella of ill health, even life-threatening disease, thought their adversity to be "a gift." We had friends and family members who suffered from cancer, stroke, and heart disease. Most of these individuals were fortunate to have beaten their illnesses, rebounded, as surgical options and treatments offered hope, cure, and, more than likely, normal life expectancies. Even those friends with AIDS saw hope for the future, improved health and extended life spans, due to the latest medications that have turned AIDS into a manageable disease. So, yes, many people dealing with disease and treatment have found new purpose in life, a deeper perspective. And, from that, they have embraced substance and found their illnesses to be a treasured gift in many ways. It is when one has those options, a viable chance, and hope of recovery, that we are all forever grateful.

But John and I rarely, if ever, heard of persons terminally ill with ALS, an always fatal disease, refer to their illness or impending death as a gift. That was the crucial difference we saw in the "gift-giving" process of disease or adversity. Those who found a new and clearer meaning due to their bouts with adversity were usually those who were blessed with the gift of hope. That, we were not afforded. There were times, however, when friends and family, in witnessing how John dealt with terminal illness with such strength, humor, and dignity, and in bearing witness to his fortitude and spirit, described it as a gift to them, a lesson not only in dying but in living as well. And this was true for all of us who watched him die, watched his daily struggles; his ability to smile, even laugh, when trapped in a motionless body, gripped with pain. Indeed, he was a gift—to all of us.

The day would proceed with myriad and varied tasks—my lists were ever present and everywhere. Caregiving for someone terminally ill and quadriplegic is a full-time job and then some. Tack on preparing meals; cleaning the house; maintaining the inside and outside; doing the laundry; juggling, ordering, and administering medications; monitoring John's health and progression; scheduling appointments with doctors, physical therapists, hospice nurses, and aides; grocery shopping; paying bills; never-ending Social Security and other medical paperwork; John's minute-by-minute needs; and then my needs—well, the days were full and exhausting. And all of this came with an indescribable heaviness of spirit, of mind and body struggling to cope, trying to survive and take care when there was no proverbial light at the end of my tunnel.

Day-to-day variations to the list would include showering John and dealing with his severe constipation. A healthy individual will go through the bathing process as quickly and effortlessly as blinking or breathing. But, for John—and me—the process was taxing and potentially dangerous. Before hospice, getting John into the handicapped shower we had installed, and from his wheelchair and onto a shower chair, was difficult and painful. At times he slipped, my strength not able to keep him from falling from the chair, and necessitating an emergency call to our friend, Parker, who, regardless of where he was or what he was doing, was there in time that could only be attributed to flight or divine intervention. On other occasions, it was my back that would become victim. Moving John with a safety belt and sliding board from wheelchair to shower chair was precarious at best. Even knowing how to bend my legs, lift properly, I would strain my back, most times to a point where it was nothing more than bothersome; other times where I was in pain and lost valuable sleep that I could not afford to lose.

When John suffered from severe constipation due to inactivity and pain medication, it could range from moderate pain and a situation we could deal with, to hospice aides in varying degrees of worry, to the need for a nurse and a moment just shy of the emergency room. Most of the time I could administer suppositories, which would take effect shortly thereafter. On more serious occasions, he would need an enema. The toilet process was not only physically exhausting for us but emotionally too, even on "good days." It would require the use of the Hoyer lift, yet again, hoisting John into the air, maneuvering him perfectly and without error over the toilet, lowering him, securing his weight onto the toilet with the lift and my guidance, then waiting. It was not the best part of the day—for either of us. Often, we could find something to joke about. And, if ever a time was needed for humor, toilet time was it. On the worst days, when John's pain was intense, his body frail and weak, he could barely hold his head up while positioned on the toilet. I would need to stand there, steadying his body with my arms so he wouldn't fall off. This was a heartbreaking sight, as his face would turn ashen, pain carved across his already hollowed cheekbones, a time that seemed to stand still.

On one particularly bad day, when the hospice aide, Sandy, and I maneuvered John onto the toilet, waited, and watched, his deterioration seemed to take a turn for the worst. The constipation was severe, and the pressure and straining on a body already broken and on its last legs appeared to be taking a potentially deadly turn. John's face turned gray, and not a gray that one associates with the living. He complained of pain, but this time not in his abdomen but rather in his chest. He was sweating profusely, his eyes barely open. Sandy, who normally could handle any situation, seemed overly concerned. When she said she needed to call Ginny, John's hospice nurse, I knew it was serious. Within minutes, Ginny arrived. A manual evacuation was painfully but successfully performed, and, thankfully, just minutes before John would have needed hospitalization. Later, however, after Ginny and I discussed the events precipitating her visit, she told me it was highly probable that John had suffered a minor heart attack. I suppose, in hindsight, I was not all that surprised. The gray pallor, the chest pain, and the profuse sweating all corroborated the possibility. And, if you knew of John's suffering—not just that day but most days—you would have secretly hoped that it might have been the end. I know John would have.

Afternoons slipped into twilight and dinner preparation, feeding John, cleaning up, and getting him ready for and back into bed. It is amazing how many things we take for granted, every waking moment of our lives, the countless unconscious actions and movements, the mundane, all of which had to be done for John. Scratching an itch, blowing his nose, drinking water, going to the bathroom, removing a lash from an eye, turning a page, adjusting a hand, a leg—a million small tasks that engrossed every minute of every day. There is little room for variation, no freedom of spontaneity. You live the same day, over and over again. You live by lists and by routine. They are a series of blurred, surreal visions—harried, exhausting, frightening, lonely, heartbreaking, strangely comforting in the familiarity, never ending, and yet, at the same time, fleeting.

Time is curious that way. It passes us by while seemingly standing still.

No, these were not the best of times. But, oddly enough, between the teeth brushing and the page turning, each day we found a moment to smile, a reason to laugh. It came naturally, somehow. But that had always been the way with our relationship. Laughter was our glue. Of course, toward the end, it became less and less. But always there was reason, however brief, to find something in the absurdity of our lives, of the world, in the perfection of nonsense — and in knowing that our lives would come together again one day — in a place where words such as pain and suffering and loss have no meaning.*

*   My heartfelt gratitude for the loving care of hospice: nurse, Ginny Poland, and aides Annette Nevells, and Sandy Nevells.

CHAPTER 16

Barefoot

*Lost, yesterday, somewhere between sunrise and sunset,
two golden hours, each set with sixty diamond minutes.
No reward is offered, for they are gone forever.*

~ Horace Mann

Up front, no one tells you all of what you may lose. Perhaps they cannot tell you everything; they simply do not know. But, when you're in the unenviable position of diagnosing terminal illness, experience and observation give you a fairly good idea. Maybe the diagnosis itself is all they feel you can bear; the impending loss of a loved one. Maybe tacking on a "by the way"—explaining that you may lose your home, savings account, and a multitude of other tangible horrors— is too much to offer, not their job. That information is readily available in pamphlets and brochures—the very ones that speak of tracheotomies and breathing ventilators, bedsores, stomach tubes, and nursing homes. Perhaps the initial numbness prevents the "by the ways" from sinking in. It's all too much to swallow, then, for fear of choking. And, soon enough, the swallowing and choking will become a reality of daily life. Tomorrow, you will forget what it was like to effortlessly swallow. You'll forget what life was like without choking.

Aside from monetary losses, perhaps the greatest losses are ones that cannot be foreseen. You may not believe it early on, but you will lose friends, lifelong friends. You will lose your future as you thought you knew it to be. You will lose freedom and spontaneity. Ultimately, and even though you may put up a good fight, you will lose all, or much, of your sense of self. Then, when you are at your most vulnerable, naked, and seemingly teetering on the edge of the earth, you will lose your spouse.

Gone, life partner. Gone, the life-affirming acts of sharing. The silent, blissful moments of just being with that one chosen person, together, watching a sunrise, a sunset; sharing a home-cooked meal; breathing deep the first breath of autumn chill, together. Hushed, unspoken moments, fleeting, tender, deep, and singularly beautiful. Gone. You will lose them all.

You will lose the slipping of a hand into yours; the comforting embrace around your trembling shoulders; the warm touch of tender lips to your own. You will lose the daily touch that we all take for granted—that all species need to thrive and nurture and to heal. Gone. Babies, of all species, must have touch. They must feel the warmth of another's touch, of their own kind or surrogate, to live, to survive. Those who go untouched often perish sooner. Young and old. Never again will I take it for granted—not a friend or stranger's embrace, a pat on the back, an unintentional brush against my arm. I want to feel it, all. It connects you to reality. It connects you with life. And now, more than any other time, when you have lost so much of it, so much living, you must cherish the smallest touch that comes your way. Grateful is how I feel when I am tenderly touched.

I could see it in John's eyes. While he could not touch me, of his own volition, I touched him a thousand times daily, and not nearly enough. Massaged, held, stroked, and kissed—the feeling of my warm, breathing skin on his made his face relax, resigned. And, when I could read in his eyes how he longed to touch me, I would gingerly lift his hand and brush it against my cheek, move his fingers through my hair. Grateful is how he felt when I touched him, when I brought his fingers, like limp petals, to my lips. Some things don't need to be spoken to be understood. And yet, every chance he could, when he still could, a tiny, whispered "thank you" parted from his lips. "You don't have to thank me," and I would smile. "Yes, I do," he'd whisper. And so I let him. It was one of the last things he could do. Thankful, we both were, for each other.

But, gradually, the sense of self begins to slip away. You are not fully aware of its fading; however, it is destined to be. Caregiving is all encompassing, consuming. Everything you do is for the one you love, the one who is dying, the taking care. Most of what is offered from those on the outside is concern for the one who is ill. Rarely, still, does one ask how you are doing. Before you know it, you are but a shadow. "I had a life once," you say to yourself. No, you have a life, still. It's just one on which you had not planned. It is like an old photograph: your life, once color, now faded shades of gray.

Presumption becomes a pinprick in your daily routine. Battling to protect the last vestiges of self, you hold tight to what you know, your gut, what you are living and breathing, day to day. Others, often well meaning, cannot resist telling you what to do, how you should feel, what to think. How can they possibly know? How can they know what is best when they have not yet walked in your shoes? Over time, there are things we think, things we think we know, and things we know. What we know usually comes from experience, hands on. All answers are not to be found in books. They cannot be found only in observation. Until one has lived the experience, breathed it, seen it minute by minute—know it for what it is, was, the small, writhing animal that it can be—no one knows for sure what is best. Please, do not presume to know. Please do not tell us how we should be feeling, how we should or shouldn't express emotion, our grief, our love, how best to survive—in your eyes. You do not know. A flip of a page or a glimpse into a window cannot offer you true insight into the depths of the unknown. When you have walked in my shoes, John's shoes, similar shoes, lost your shoes, then, only then, will you have a sense of the experience. Until that moment, presumption, although well meaning and perhaps heartfelt, is a painful pinprick, an abrasion on the remains of one's sense of self, caregiver, or the dying. That is my story from my experience. As Keats wrote, "Nothing ever becomes real till it is experienced—Even a proverb is no Proverb to you till your Life has illustrated it."

When you are barefoot, then the things you think you know, you will know.

CHAPTER 17

In the Blink of an Eye

The moon is down.

~ Shakespeare

Silence

When he would cry, he was silent. His face was not unlike a newborns — scrunched and folded, red, swollen, mouth wide open and wet, eyes tight. And, for that long, breathless moment, no sound. But, with John, there was no blood-curdling scream following that terrible pause. Like Edvard Munch's painting, John's scream was silent. And, as I learned, the silent wail is far more horrific than the audible.

Hands
nobody, not even the rain, has such small hands

~ e.e. cummings

What I noticed first about John were his hands. They were the most beautiful hands I had ever seen: large, angular, sculpted as if carved from stone. They were lovely. At the end, though, his hands became foreign; someone else's hands had replaced his once-strong ones. Now, these hands were small and thin. They were white, almost a bluish-white really, long and narrow, without muscle or strength; more like a woman's hands, fragile and soft. They lay slack at his sides or wherever he asked me to place them. On the tops of his thighs; he liked them there, warm. He laughed once at how rough and strong my hands felt now, his being so very sensitive to their touch. So, as I once again moved his paralyzed hands, I was even more aware of their delicacy, of the strange beauty in their lifelessness, their almost ethereal sheen, and I tried to remember what they looked like so long ago: strong, able, and pulsing with life.

Life, now

Can't walk, can't move, can't dress myself. Can't speak, can't swallow without choking, can't pick up the cat, can't go to the bathroom, can't blow my nose, brush my teeth, scratch an itch. Can't say hello, can't say I love you, can't play my guitar, scatter birdseed, touch your skin, hold your hand, can't say it will be okay. Can barely smile when I want to laugh. Can still cry silent, wet tears but without sound. Can nod my head but with some pain. Can try with all my might to communicate my gratefulness, my love, my sorrow, my friendship, and my will to live. Can be held without holding. Can accept a loving embrace with much gratitude but even greater loss. Can close my eyes and dream of better times. Can dream of limbs moving freely and fluidly, without pain. Can dream of running, making love, grasping a hand, moving my arm around a shoulder, pulling up my pants, lifting a fork to my lips, swirling wine in its glass, stroking the cat, peeling an orange, strumming strings, turning the page of a book, brushing the hair from your eyes — all things good and worth remembering. Can still love and be loved. But even that cannot make life worth living when you know it is time to say No More. When the reality of the Cants overweighs the memories of the Cans, and the unbearable pain makes even the most beautiful of past Cans seem blurred and harder to recall. Then, the final strength comes in the decision to let go. To let go of living on memories. To let go of the faces you love so deeply that it feels like a swift kick in the gut. To let go of all earthly things that once were beautiful and held hope, all you knew and cherished. To let go of all that one knows, completely, without reservation; to give way to the unknown, and say goodbye to all familiar and warm. To close one's eyes and embrace what comes next with dignity and grace and the knowledge that you accomplished all that was truly important — to love and be loved and to be good. Then, sleep comes naturally, thick with Cans. Forever awaits in some new place, perhaps not so far away after all. So tired of all the Cannots. So ready to toss them aside; to shed this heaviness of skin and bone and all those memories, and swim with light, strong limbs through weightless clouds. I've let go because I Can. It is the last thing that I can do.

Care

... so intimate that when I fall asleep your eyes close.

~ Pablo Neruda

"John, you okay?" I would call out from another room, just to make sure. "Yes," he would answer, so small I could catch it in the palm of my hand.

Flight

A robin redbreast in a cage sets all heaven in a rage.

~ William Blake

Many times, I felt like that robin. "That's me," I thought, "a trapped bird." A free spirit, barely still, but free enough to feel the bars, on the worst of days; the trappings of all that responsibility, the losses, the corners that were getting closer and closer each moment. And where would I have flown had that cage door been opened? Where would my wings have taken me? I would have probably circled the rooftop, the yard; flown high above the cove and reach, taking in the fresh bite of salt air, the smells of the earth, the warmth of the sun across my feathers, hovering in midair as I gazed longingly at the horizon; then, quietly, resigned by the pull of my own heartstrings, I would have flown Home, to John, from where I began.

Answers Not Yet for the Knowing

What are you thinking while you lie there dying? Are you thinking those profound thoughts that only the healthy, the not terminal suppose that a dying man thinks? Things we cannot possibly comprehend, the meaning of life, whether it all was worth it, the summing up and evaluation of all that was said and done? Or is it more feeling the dying process? Does the mind slow down to allow one to truly feel, perhaps for the first time, the systematic rhythms of the body; the pumping of blood through the veins; the beating of one's heart; the tingling of the skin; the sound of one's breath; of all organs, churning, pulsing,

162

doing one last gig before the final curtain? When you lie there so still, so quiet, gazing skyward, eyes fixed and glassy, and I walk into the room, and you seem startled by the intrusion, what was happening for you? Do you think only of death? Of letting go? Of whether it will hurt, of what I will see? Of what comes afterward? Whether those I leave behind will be okay? Or are you so far past that point that you see and feel only rocking; the primordial cradle of waves and warmth and darkness. Are you comforted? Are you okay? That is what I need to know. Selfishly too, I want to know more than that. I want to know what you are just beginning to know. What I will not know until I, like you, lay dying. Is there a wonderful release when you finally let go? A warm blanket of freedom that suddenly caresses you once you've said, "It is time"? Does the brain, your thinking, resort to a place, a plane, which only functions as a home for acceptance, love, release, freedom from the prison of a dying body, of this world? Do you see things differently? Do you see different things? Do you see loved ones who have gone before you? Can you feel them, can you hear them, are they calling you to join them? You didn't know if there was anything after death. You told me so. I wanted to believe that you believed there was something. "I'm not sure," you said. "I don't know." How could you? But you promised me you would let me know, somehow, someway. "Let me know, John," I whispered. You nodded that you would and gave me a look so foreign, so far from anything I have ever seen or understood, that I knew if you could, you would keep your promise. I think you were perhaps more surprised than I. You kept your promise. And, while you gave me the gift of "knowing" that there is indeed life, a force, an energy, a spirit (what do you call this?) after the body is gone, you gave me an insight that not everyone has been given. Now I know. Now I know it's true. And perhaps the greatest gift of all is not being afraid. In the knowing, I am not as fearful. That is one of the greatest gifts you gave to me.

Faraway

Toward the end and during the most difficult days, daydreams and fantasies were the tiny secrets I kept in my pocket. So tired, so helpless, when all chores and responsibilities were done, for now, I would reach into my pocket and pull from my handful of polished stones that were my daydreams. If only for a moment, I could close my eyes and hold onto those little stones, and transport myself to someplace faraway where everything was easy and good. By holding my lids tight, I could get just enough dream darkness to pretend that I was happy and hopeful, that I was suddenly young, beautiful, filled with life and endless possibility. I wanted to remember what it was like to be held, to hold, to let go of the weight of thought and process and just be. I would dream of making love again, sometimes with John, sometimes not, with anyone who could hold me and make me forget. Daydreams and fantasies are mostly to help us forget. They are our secrets, our safety nets, our crutches when the real world has failed us or crippled us of our options. These journeys were safe and far enough away so not to harm. I was often on a beach — a lovely, white beach — or in the African bush, surrounded by the sounds of the wild and the heady scent of flora and fauna. I would lie on my back, limp, looking skyward, into the clouds that we always hope will hold all answers to all questions. Drunk by the sun, bathed in the perfume of flowering trees and grasses, I would be made love to by a faceless stranger, whom I loved and who loved me. I wanted to feel the strength and heaviness of a body on top of mine again, to remember what it felt like to feel the freedom of passivity, such abandon, such lightness of spirit. I wanted to feel, but only tactile feelings, my head aching from so much thinking and taking care. With my body neglected and my brain working overtime, I longed to be lulled into the softness and warmth of skin and waves and breath. And, as quickly as those tiny stones were pulled out, they were tucked away, into their dark places. And, as I opened my lids, the harsh light of my day would sting my eyes and, for now, flood the oasis of beach and bushwillows.

One Last Dance

It was a night of full moon and blankets of snow. Past midnight, I looked outside onto the landscape bathed in moonlight and remembered how John loved these nights. Full moonlight would cast a bluish tint across an otherwise white landscape, a dreamscape of sorts, otherworldly, of the moon and stars, foreign, hushed, fleeting. And, as I looked across the vastness of blue and shadow, I quietly sang to myself, "… and dance by the light of the moon," and wondered if, when I turned around, John would suddenly appear, out in the snow, beneath the full moon and bare birches, dancing, twirling, making snow angels beneath the stars. I hoped so. In my mind's eye, I could see it clearly. And the next morning when I awoke, I strained my neck to look out across the deep cover of snow, looking for footprints or angel wings beneath the crabapples. The snow pack was unblemished, but maybe his feather-light wings had not touched the ground.

CHAPTER 18

The Perception of Fog

Fear death? — to feel the fog in my throat,
The mist in my face.

~ Robert Browning

It is September 23, 2001. Barely two weeks since 9/11 and the terrorist attacks in New York and Washington. I am on Deer Isle, in a small rental cabin on the sea. Across the bridge from my home and just minutes away, John spends time with his sister, Lis, and brother, Clay. It is the last time they will see each other. John's health is failing, his energy low, voice and body weak, his life fading. He is confined to a wheelchair. Siblings together. They are saying their goodbyes, privately. I leave them, brothers and sister, and take these two days of solitude along a desolate stretch of beach.

I am lonely and frightened. Two weeks ago seemingly changed everything. I am frightened of losing John, of his impending death; now, with the world in such turmoil and uncertainty, my life feels more unsure than ever. The loneliness I feel is palpable. I can taste it. The quiet aches. I need life around me, energy, some token of normalcy. I sit, looking out in the direction of the sea. I can hear the waves crashing, the foghorns in the distance, the clang of the buoys. Before me is a wall of fog—porous, intangible, yet no less a wall. Hidden too are the towering evergreens and deciduous trees, now losing their leaves; I can hear the wind shaking them loose and falling to an imaginary ground. A melancholy loon, invisible, calls out in the ghostly mist.

The singular vision of a solid reality is my feet before me, propped up on a weathered deck rail. In this dreamscape, only the senses of smell and hearing, and basic instinct, outweigh vision, perception, and balance. If suspended in midair, I would not know up from down. It is that kind of fog. It swallows you whole. Somehow, this blurred perception, this enveloping white wall, the very sense of being absorbed, all seem appropriate for my life now. Not even the surest of beings can be all that certain in fog. And my life is anything but certain. My horizon is missing.

I strain to see even a hint of shape behind the white wall: a blurred line, anything. But any sense of solid is impossible. I punch my fists—straight into the wall—and find only space on the other side. I come away with nothing. Not even pain from the punching, a hint of being alive. I am sad, needing to know what lies on the other side. For no other reason than human beings need to know what surrounds them, what lies ahead, for better or worse.

Sad, I stand up and turn around. I look up, over the shingled gray roof of my cabin, and am surprised to see what had been sitting patiently behind me. A ceiling of blue. It is as if an imaginary boundary has been drawn where the wall of fog and blue would meet, clean and sure, no fuzzy edges, no watering of line where one begins and the other ends. So alone in my sadness, blue appears behind me. This seems an optimistic metaphor for my life. Frightened, unsure of what tomorrow will bring, uncertain about my future without John, some sense deep within my being tells me that life will be brighter, someday. In all the darkness and fog, the cloudiness of spirit, clarity will ease its way through and out of the dense fog— blue will prevail. At this moment, cold, damp, lonely, and sad, grasping fistfuls of fog, I know one day the ceiling of blue will ground me.

CHAPTER 19

Solitary Confinement

Here is no water but only rock.

~ Thomas Stearns Eliot

Solitary confinement comes in many forms. And all bad. I cannot pretend to know or understand what mandated imprisonment feels like, to be behind bars and forced to exist alone. I don't believe anyone should live a life alone. Man is a social animal for the most part. Being alone for too long, or a lifetime, is not good for one's soul. Naturally, there are exceptions to the rule, but few and far between.

I have seen, however, a different form of imprisonment that surely qualifies as a form of living hell. The form of solitary confinement was imposed by terminal illness, a crippling disease. This incarceration I witnessed firsthand, but not as the unfortunate victim. And he was a victim in a singularly horrific way.

Trapped body.

This solitary place was an entrapment, a cell; a suffocating prison with walls, floor, and ceiling, bearing down upon one's psyche. We do not have to touch these walls to feel the power and weight of their confinement. A cell is a cell, whether created from a paralyzed body or societal mandates.

My husband's prison was his body. Paralyzed from ALS, he lived in a motionless body of skin and bone, unable to move even a finger, trapped alive by a disease that leaves only an active and vital mind to function in a sea of stillness. For days and months, which eventually bled into years, I watched as my husband's body continued to waste away. A quadriplegic, I saw his cell become smaller and smaller each day. A prisoner within his own body, his cell not of cement walls but of dead muscle and useless limbs. From a brain that screamed, "Move!" a body ignored and lay frozen. Did he feel like an animal caught in a steel trap? On the most unbearable of days, did the trapped mind envision the gnawing off, the severing of the caught limb to escape the torment? Better free than trapped? That is what I saw, some days. A caught animal.

I do not believe in suffering. Sometimes, one will do whatever it takes to be free. Sometimes, one says in a voice so small it is almost invisible, "I think it's time to go." Sometimes, we have to watch those we love free themselves from their solitary confinement. It is not always easy to accept the emptiness of the steel trap, no matter how horrific it was. Empty or not, it claims its victim.

We tend to compare. We presume one form of suffering to be worse than another. Some will argue that it is far worse to deal with a failing mind coupled with a healthy body. Others will say it is far more ghastly to have a vital brain and a crippled body. We assume, compare, weigh, and measure. But, in truth, nothing good comes from prolonged suffering, no matter how it is dealt. Whether from a dying body or a mind that wreaks havoc, they are all painful places. They are small and dark. Perhaps, worst of all, they are lonely. And, no matter how much we want to enter these dark, lonely places of those we love, we can only bear witness from the sidelines.

CHAPTER 20

When It Is Time to Go

... Like glimpses of forgotten dreams.

~ Tennyson

I will forever remember those words; the last of tiny, white petals to bloom from his soft, pink lips. How they shot over and through me—not a rain of flowers but a torrent of water, engulfed by waves. I remember the numbness, the fighting for my breath, as I felt the sea pull me under, my need to repeat the words, seemingly through mouthfuls of sand, when, in fact, they were as clear and as deafening as any words ever spoken.

"I think it's time to go."

"It's time to go? Okay—" I said, in a voice I did not recognize. A voice as fragile as cracked glass, as surprised as a newborn. No matter how hard you try, no matter how much you think you've prepared, you can never be. Not for those words. How can you? They are the beginning of the next world, the ending of another—only one of which you can be a part. At that moment, again, the universe has changed. Shifted. Hold on! You know what the next wave will bring, the power and force of its energy. It will take you under, swallow you low into its belly, if you don't find your anchor. Now is the time. Toss it over, and let it settle, deep.

He nodded, weakly. His face resigned, sad from the words, the finality of his decision, the letting go.

From what depths does one pull in finding the strength to utter those words? How does one feel when the final decision is made, when the leaving behind, however painful, is far more preferable and right than the unknown?

I had never seen him look so sad. Even in the freedom of decision, of releasing himself from stillness and torment, his eyes were shadowed with sorrow. But, as the days went on, that would change. The color that began to bloom in his hollowed cheeks was that of acceptance, of peace. There were some days when he would smile. No bodily movement, no voice, just a small blooming of the lips—a flower, one last time from this earth. Was the flower for me? Or was it what he was just beginning to know, as his new door opened little by little each day?

He stopped eating. That was how he would release himself, let go. In a body that had nearly disappeared, frail, shattered, weighing almost nothing at all, it still took 13 days. Thirteen days before he joined the wind—blowing like dandelion spore, riding the thermals on a wish. His wish.

It is hard to go about your business when your husband is dying in the next room. Does he smell the food I prepare for myself? Does it make the starving process all the more difficult, to resist sustenance, resist life? It took me a couple of days to fully digest that one—the different dynamics playing out in each room, the sheer determination of each of us separated only by a narrow threshold—one of survival, the other of death. But I had to eat. I had to retain my strength, my health. Somehow, amidst the turmoil of the last few years, I remained strong, my health intact. I could not falter now. I still had things to take care of: John, his final wishes, and my life. If only one of us was to survive, then I would walk away as strong and as unscathed as I possibly could.

As I look back on those last days—on my questions, concerns, and heartbreak over the processes of living and dying—I realize that much of what plagued me were the philosophical questions and angst of a healthy human being. When one is dying, when one has made the decision to release himself from disease or illness, the mind must surely function in a way that we cannot comprehend. It is not ours to understand. One evening, I asked John if the smell of my dinner bothered him, made it more difficult. He smiled and whispered, "No." There appeared to be no internal struggle of want or need for food. The ideas of sustenance, hunger, or satiation were no longer part of John's world. When I accepted this, to the degree where one can understand such a foreign concept, I was able to abandon the feelings of guilt, despair, the need to feed and nurture him, even though I knew it could not or should not be.

Each day, a new wave rolled over me. When I felt myself going under, I would slip onto the deck, if only for a short while, and regain my footing from the temple of nature that surrounded me. Always, the natural world had sustained me; now, more than ever, as my husband lay dying, as my closest friends and family were thousands of miles away, nature's reassuring embrace kept me grounded and forever grateful. I missed the sound of voices, of interaction, of the days when John and I would engage in hours of effortless discussion about everything and nothing at all. But, in exchange for lost voices, I received the gift of birdsong; of wind rustling through leaves; the gentle lapping of waves along the cove; the delicate rift of butterfly, bee, and hummingbird wings. I watched the rosa rugosas seemingly explode overnight with hot pink roses. The deep-purple lupine in the lower field grew tall and sturdy. The crabapple blossoms came and went; the lilac bush filled the house with sweet perfume; a multitude of fledglings flew in and out of the garden, testing their wings, the miracle of flight. And, always, there was Africa. In my spiritual connection with nature, the world outside my doors, the reminder and memories of Africa were always close to the surface and yet nearest to my heart.

A week into John's decision to stop eating, he asked to get out of bed one last time. He wanted to watch our wedding video, he told me. It was the last request he made. The hospice nurse did not think he should be removed from bed, too precarious and painful at this stage, and she offered to bring her own small television and VCR to our home, to the bedroom, and set it up so we could view it from John's hospital bed. But he would not have it. Once more, he wanted to be taken from his bed, sit upright in the world, and watch a video we had not seen since our wedding day, nearly 11 years earlier.

I remember the last time I lifted him from his bed. I hoisted his small body into the air, his limbs and head hanging limp like a rag doll. I wheeled him into the sitting room where I had everything ready for the screening. The wheelchair seemed to swallow him, a wisp of a body, more of bone and loose flesh than anything else, his head way too large now and out of proportion, barely able to balance itself on a slackened neck. I sat next to him. I held his hand. We watched ourselves, younger and healthier then, filled with joy, laughter, and so much hope. He saw his sister and brother, our family and friends. We watched ourselves embrace and kiss beneath a stand of ancient redwoods near the sea, in the City by the Bay.

He wept. I choked back tears as I held him tighter, tenderly securing my arms around him, one last time.

Everything then was for the last time.

What came next, and through our tears, caught us both off guard. We had forgotten that, following the wedding day videotape, was footage of our first date some 15 years before, taken by a friend as we attended the annual Renaissance Faire in Marin County. How young we looked, then. How beautiful he looked. I had forgotten how beautiful he once was. I heard his voice again—clear, strong, yet soft as silk. I saw his healthy, strong body move freely and fluidly. I saw the exuberance of life in his pale-blue eyes; hope for the future on our younger, innocent faces. Innocence is a marvelous thing. It is good not to know too much of what lies ahead, how abruptly the world can end, the edge and drop oftentimes closer than one would like.

We wept together. We wept for those days, for happier times. We wept over the loss of his body, his voice, and our future. But, most of all, we wept for the strength of our love. We had not been afforded the gift of time, of hopes and dreams, of growing old with one another. But rather we were blessed with a love that had endured and blossomed in the hardest of times, sustained us through disease, and, even at death, was a bond greater than any other we had ever known. As we often said, our time may have been cut short, but what we had, together, most people do not find in a lifetime.

I wheeled him back to bed. His blue eyes were red and swollen. I kissed him. He fell asleep quickly and peacefully.

In watching him sleep, I felt a small wave caress my body. This one was gentle and warm. It rocked me, easily, pooled around my ankles, then slipped out to sea.

CHAPTER 21

The Morning Before

Come forth into the light of things,
Let Nature be your teacher.

~ Wordsworth

The morning before John died, I saw a bear. In the 10 years we had lived in Maine, we had never seen a bear. We had heard stories, over the years, of neighbors who had seen bears in their yards in the light of early morning. We had even found bear scat dropped around our driveway, thick with blueberries, a sure sign, but never a sighting. As lovers of wildlife, we always felt a bit shortchanged at their elusiveness.

That morning at early dawn, the light still pink from a rising sun, John's hospice nurse, Ginny, arrived. As she had done the last few days and would continue to do for as long as needed, she would arrive at the house at daybreak and return at dusk to assist me in administering John's medication. He was comatose at this point, and I knew it was only a matter of hours before he would let go, escaping the torment of a paralyzed body wracked with pain.

This day, however, was different. Ginny rushed into the kitchen obviously excited over something. I had just gotten up and was putting the kettle on the stove. "There's a bear in your yard," she gasped. "It is just off your porch near the rugosas." I don't think I even said hello or good morning. At that moment, the bear was far more important than a simple greeting, and I rushed to the front door. Just as I opened the door and stood behind the screen, the young bear, perhaps two years old, climbed up the porch steps only to meet me eye to eye. There were perhaps 3 feet that separated us, and, for what seemed like a very long time, we just stared. I think the small bear was as surprised as I was at our meeting. It was lovely and as beautiful a creature as I had ever seen. I wanted to look at it forever, absorb everything about it. But, when I realized it wasn't moving away or frightened, I did what I had to do. I yelled, clapped my hands, and shouted, "Go!" Only then did it lumber off the porch and, in a swirl of bulk and soft fur, disappear into the pines. I knew all too well that at this time of year, bears — just coming out of hibernation, hungry, and often with cubs — scrounge and scavenge for any available food. Birdfeeders, trash cans, blueberry barrens, anything that holds promise is fair game until a homeowner pulls out a gun and forever ends the bear's hunger. It happens time and time again. I had no choice but to frighten off the bear. The last thing I wanted was this beautiful animal to feel any sense of comfort or ease around a human being. Even me.

In a matter of seconds, it was over. My first encounter with a Maine bear, and just an arm's length away. I couldn't help but feel that this was an omen of sorts — a sign, a signal, a wonderful gift meant solely for me. I went into our bedroom and put my lips to John's ear. His breathing was shallow, his eyes closed. "John," I whispered. "There was a bear on our porch, a young bear!" I felt a rush of excitement and, regardless of whether or not he could hear me, I was going to tell him about what I had seen. They say the hearing is the last thing to go. I like to believe he heard me. His breathing did seem to change slightly; it became faster, and I thought I saw his eyes flutter beneath their lids.

A few friends told me that this sighting was amazing in many respects. One, who had studied Native American animal totems or spirits, thought the encounter was indeed meaningful. The bear represents introspection, she said, strength and healing. During hibernation, in its dark cave, the bear takes the time to think, to feel, to make sense out of its situation, and, ultimately, to heal. From this time, alone in its cave, the bear gains wisdom and strength. When it emerges into the sunlight, it is older and wiser, ready to move forward, into the light. The bear represents a strong healing power, perhaps the strongest healing power of all the animal totems.

I too had been through a hibernation of sorts. Alone, in my cave, in the surrounding darkness of John's illness and impending death, I had spent much time reflecting, giving way to hopes and dreams for a day when I could step outside once again, into the light of a new world, moving forward. In all the enveloping darkness, I had never lost hope. After all, even in tragedy, our bond was all about love. And from the depth of that love came an inner strength, for both of us, which carried us through.

The morning before John died, I saw a bear. It was the first time. I have not seen one since.

CHAPTER 22

The Last Night

Somewhere the Sky touches the Earth,
and the name of that place is the End.

~ African saying (Wakamba)

There was a storm that evening. From what the hospice nurse had told me, and from what I could see, John would likely die during the night. We rarely lost power, but, this night— John's last—the thunderstorm downed the power lines, and I sat alone in the dark. I lit a few candles and an oil lamp, and pulled John's wheelchair alongside his hospital bed. I sat in it. Beneath me, I could feel the curves and depressions he had worn in the seat. I couldn't help but laugh, albeit weakly, at the idea that I was sitting in the dark, and there was no power. There was much I had yet to do, to take care of if John died this night, and not having electricity would make it all the more complicated.

His medication had been administered: a low dose of oxycontin. John chose not to have morphine or even a higher dose of oxycontin. As he had told me many times, he didn't want to spend his final days in oblivion. He wanted to feel, to experience his last days of life, even if it meant dealing with excruciating pain. At this point though, John, unconscious, was comfortable and no longer in pain. Barely alive, a frame more skeletal than human, John's body had deteriorated to nothing more than a mass of excess skin and protruding bone. We guessed his weight to be no more than 70 pounds, probably much less. His 5-foot, 10-inch frame seemed to have shrunk. He looked small and fragile, yet his head and hands seemed too large now and no longer suited his frail body.

My lists were nearby. There were things to be tended to, John's final wishes. I was relaxed, somewhat. I suppose, at that moment, just hours before the end of all I once knew, a sense of calm prevailed as there was nothing left for me to do but wait. Only after his passing would the taking care begin yet again. I had approximately one hour following John's death to spend with him, privately, before I had to make the calls.

Upon John's passing, time would be critical. After his diagnosis, we agreed to sign papers that would allow John's brain, muscle, and spinal tissue to be harvested and used for ALS research. We were fortunate to have one of the leading ALS doctors in the country, and I knew the protocol that must be followed to ensure that John's tissue was promptly removed and sent to the labs in Massachusetts. Because of this time frame, I had much to take care of in a rather short period. A few days before, I had contacted the appropriate doctor in Bangor who would remove John's tissue samples. I notified John's doctor and research assistants in Boston as well, letting them know that the samples would shortly be en route. Autopilot. A life too surreal to be anything other than a dream.

Shortly after 10 o'clock, the power came back on. For the next couple of hours, I sat next to John's bedside; his thin, damp hand in mine. I talked to him. I told him things that are only spoken once in a lifetime, singular words of comfort and love and of deep gratitude. I thanked him. I watched — watched how his body went through the final stages, the transformation: the limbs that first went cold; the change in coloring; his breathing; the beads of sweat that collected on his forehead, upper lip, and eyelids as his head burned with heat while his feet turned to ice, and from white to blue. It was not so bad, really. There was a strange and comforting peacefulness about it, about the dying process. We are so fearful of death and dying. Yet, to see it up close, to tenderly touch it and breathe it, to experience it in all its strange, ethereal beauty and naturalness was something I had not expected. I was not afraid. After many years of illness, I had accompanied John to this final moment. I had cared for him at home. And now, with his fading hand in mine, watching him die in his own room, beneath a roof that had held so many joyful memories. He had the person next to him who loved him most, and, as his life slipped away, I could feel his energy emanate into my own. He would forever be part of me now. I felt fortunate.

When I could no longer keep my eyes open, I climbed into bed. Our bed, once. I had pushed it into the middle of the room to be just inches from his rented hospital bed. I could not sleep. I tossed and turned for some time, anxious, my skin prickling. Then, suddenly, I could not breathe. I was beginning to panic. The sounds of John's quiet, shallow breathing became deafening as I could not catch my own breath. I pulled my pillow over my head in attempts to drown out the sound of the shallow breathing beside me that, for whatever reason, was suffocating my own breath. For a moment, I felt as though I would go crazy — couldn't breathe, pulsating sound was roaring all around me — and then, abruptly, it stopped. I felt a sudden numbness. I removed the pillow from my face. I caught a deep breath. I called out to the dark. "John?" I whispered. What had I expected to hear back? His voice had silenced long before. I knew. But, even in the knowing, one last time I had to say his name. Out loud.

I turned on the light. He was still and silent. I sat on the edge of my bed and let out a few muffled cries and moans, and then I said to the air, the room, "Thank God it's over!" I wept again but only for a moment. Relief. The long suffering was over. For both of us. I stood up and held his limp hand. I smiled at a face that, even in death, was kind and gentle and, finally, at peace. Tenderly, as if touching a newborn bird, over partially opened eyes, I smoothed his eyelids down and shut. They were warm and moist. I lit a candle. I turned on the radio near John's bedside and let soft, classical notes dance around the room. I noted the time, wrote it down. I removed John's wedding band lest I forget in all the rush of thought and emotion and things that needed to be done. I pulled a pair of small scissors from the bureau and snipped three wavy locks of hair. He had such beautiful hair. I smelled each one, took in a deep breath of scent from his curls — John's smell. I removed his catheter and washed him gently with warm water. I massaged lavender-scented lotion into his withered skin. I kissed him, lightly and for the last time, on his forehead. He was gone.

The first call was to Ginny. She was on her way. She would notify the funeral home, the caretaker who would transport John's body to the medical lab in Bangor. The next call was to Parker, one of John's closest friends and my crutch through the worst of days, the final days in caring for John. Ginny arrived first. She held me tight; I held even tighter. Shortly after, Parker arrived. He made sure I was okay, then asked if he could see John.

The morning unfolded into a beautiful June day. In the early-morning air, two osprey soared over the rooftop, circling and screeching. They circled above the house for some time, their cries louder and louder. As the screeching became nearly deafening, we stepped onto the deck and watched them soar — it was as if they were bidding a final farewell, a tribute to a man who loved all things wild. John loved the osprey. Each May, when they would arrive back in Maine from their wintering grounds as far south as Latin America, we would get in the car and find the handful of osprey nests dotting the Blue Hill peninsula — just to see — see if they had returned, unscathed.

The air was filled with birdsong. The rosa rugosas were in full bloom, and lupine choked the fields below. The new sun was gentle and warm. A soft breeze lifted off the waters of the reach and cove. The three of us — Ginny, Parker, and I — stood on the deck and looked up, out, and around, and at each other. No words were spoken; none were needed. It was perhaps the most beautiful morning we had ever seen.

The pair of osprey, who circled overhead at the news of John's death, stayed. They built an immense nest, an architectural gem, at the top of a massive pine on the land next door. From our deck, each summer, the nest is in perfect sight. The osprey soar and screech, fly in and out with fish from the cove tight in their talons. I can see their every move: their mating rituals, feeding, the caring of their young. They have been here for three years.

For me, nests represent hope. They represent life, a future, and new beginnings. The osprey began building this nest on the morning John died. June 27, 2002. I am watching them now.*

---

* From the initial diagnosis in Bangor to the definitive in Boston two and a half years later, John lived for six years with ALS.

CHAPTER 23

On the Wings of a Wave

*… wherever you go, that's wherever you
are, and nobody knows it but me …*

~ Anon.

In the 10 years we had lived in Maine, John never returned to California. Now, I was taking him back, from where we began, and for the last time. At the onset of his illness, he had told me where he wanted his ashes to be scattered, between two beloved places, close to his heart. Limantour Spit at the Point Reyes National Seashore and part of the greater Pacific Ocean, and along the pristine sailing passage of Eggemoggin Reach from which our home in Maine looked out.

Before I knew John, he had lived in Point Reyes, just north of San Francisco in Marin County. He had loved it there — a remote wilderness where gentle slopes and rolling hills dotted with oaks, sagebrush, and wildflowers tumbled into an often wild sea. Back then, cattle ranches and dairy farms were plentiful, and John took pleasure in riding horses along the hillsides and headlands. But it was Limantour Spit that nurtured his soul: the empty stretch of beach, silent except for the calls of seabirds and gently lapping waves, or storm-riddled dunes, where relentless winds and crashing surf met in a convergence of powerful energy. It was there, in this magical place — where land met sea; where the sky, sandy beach, and marshlands teemed with cormorants and albatross, osprey, and great blue herons — that John wanted to be, a final resting place, his energy forever part of the winds and waves of the coastal plain.

Six months after his death, I flew back to California. With three of my closest friends, and on a clear, warm November morning, we crossed the Golden Gate Bridge and drove to the secluded foothills that terraced the protected salt marshes and beaches giving way to the sea. The beach, for the most part, was empty. Gulls and terns gingerly danced and pecked at succulent morsels exposed along the flats. There was a warm breeze coming off the ocean, a brilliant blue sky illuminated the water's surface and created diamond crystals in the sand. We took off our shoes and felt the still, cool sand seep through our toes. It could not have been a more perfect day to give John back to the timelessness of the sea.

We rolled up our pant legs. Together, with handfuls of ashes that I had mixed with lavender buds and rose petals, we walked into the foamy, cool surf. We tossed him into the air, the waves, smiling, laughing, the perfection of the moment and the happiness he had brought into our lives, filling us with an unexpected joy. He flew above, settled, and rolled over with the waves. He became one with the sea and the sky, the dunes and salt marshes. The pulse of the sea beat even stronger that day.

This summer in Maine, he will join the reach and, ultimately, with the ebb and flow of tides, ride the gentle currents into the Atlantic. He will swim with light, strong limbs through familiar oceans that straddle the land, and then, laughing at the freedom of his weightlessness and motion, he will swim on—into deeper seas, from where all life began.

CHAPTER 24

The Small Gifts We Hold Close

No act of kindness, no matter
how small, is ever wasted.

~ Aesop

Shortly after John's death, I received a letter from a friend from San Francisco. Over the years, Dick and his wife, Nancy, were exceptional friends to us. They had visited our home in Maine, and we had spent time with them in their second home in Lancaster, Pennsylvania. While I received many heartfelt tributes to John, this letter in particular summed up so much of John's spirit, his strength as a friend and as a thinker, and the unique beauty of our relationship. I have held it close ever since.

July 5, 2002

Dear Jan,

I know you have been through one of the most trying and heroic events a person can go through, but through these past few years, as Nancy and I thought of you and John working through this trial together, the image of your loving face seemed to hold the whole picture together for me. It seemed so fitting that John, in his last request, wanted to view the video of your wedding.

For us, it was a sustaining honor to have shared in some of the quality of your relationship with John. Among especially successful relationships, yours was very special.

I will always remember the first time I met John. I was to work on your ceilings at your home in the Castro, and John and I began talking about Francis Fukuyama's, The End of History and the Last Man.

The sensation of quick, honest exchange, along with his wonderful fascination with thought of any sort, created a mutual respect and abiding interest that will always remain with me.

In some of these images taken from Nancy's photos of our day in Castine together, I see reminders of conversation with John which were as personally penetrative and openly speculative as any in my life. It was an experience that gave me clarity about doing Hospice volunteering which I have been doing for about four years now.

I am sure you have received testimony about John's wonderful spirit from many people, and I want to add to that sincere praise: How I loved his humor and light spirit! His fast readiness to tackle any idea, his facility in seeing the seemingly opposite side of anything.

I remember his often joking about what he might do "when he would grow up," when, in fact, he had done more growing than most men could hope for.

I just want to tell you, Jan, of my tremendous respect for John, and how my experience of him will remain one of the guides for me in the remainder of my life.

Love, Dick

CHAPTER 25

Q&A: An Etiquette Primer on Death & Dying

A jest breaks no bones.

~ Samuel Johnson

Heartfelt eloquence was not always the case, however. And there were the clumsier moments when friends were unintentionally hurtful or dismissive, which could only be acknowledged with the understanding that we all trip up now and again, especially in uncomfortable situations. Sometimes it's better to say nothing at all. The following are examples of a few comments made to either John or me after his diagnosis and what not to say to those dealing with terminal illness.

Q: Is it okay to say to a friend or family member recently diagnosed with a terminal disease, "Well, we all have to go sometime ..." Or, a variation thereof, "Well, we're all going to die. That's a fact of life."

A: No. There is no need to point out that we will all die at some point. This we already know. What the above comments do are dismiss, negate, and trivialize the depth of seriousness of terminal disease. The dying person and his partner are devastated in ways you cannot imagine. They are wracked with raw emotion, confusion, fear of the unknown, isolation borne from disease, and the loss of future, particularly if someone is diagnosed at a relatively young age. The last thing they need is the most profound experience of their lives reduced to less than it is.

Q: Is it okay to say to someone terminally ill and facing months or years of suffering and crippling symptoms, "Thank God it wasn't sudden, like a heart attack. That's the most horrible fate imaginable. Even the Bible says to die in one's sleep is the worst possible fate ..."

A: No. Can anyone compare? Each case is different, individual, and tragic in its own right. Yes, it would be and is horrific to lose a loved one through sudden death, as I've been a part of. But to say to someone who is facing the impending death of a spouse—a slow, dying process drawn out by paralysis, the possibility of choking to death, a voice that will cease, breathing and stomach tubes, all of which fit snuggly under the heading of "prolonged suffering"—that it is a far better fate than say, a heart attack? Well, I would take the heart attack. No one wants to see a loved one suffer. At one point, John's doctor was making a house call as he was quadriplegic and could no longer leave the house. His symptoms were worsening, and John, still with a sense of humor intact, said, "I would have paid good money to have had a heart attack." He laughed but meant it. His father had died of a heart attack in his 30s, and John always thought he might follow suit. The doctor, seeing his deterioration, knowing of his excruciating pain, nodded and said, "I bet you do." As did I. We simply can't presume one is worse than the other; it's all difficult.

Q: Is it okay to say to someone recently told they are going to die, "Hey, you're not dying! You look perfectly healthy to me!" Or, "You look fine to me. Your doctors don't know what they're talking about!"

A: No. Those dealing with terminal illness have endured countless tests, hospital visits, biopsies, and both the trauma and eventual acceptance (as best they can) of coming to terms with death. They have gone through an emotional roller coaster. Please don't set them back by saying it "ain't so." It's okay to be positive and upbeat. But there are many other ways to express that optimism without feigned or actual denial. It would be better—or at least more honest—to say something such as, "Hey, you look pretty good for a dead guy!" (Well, maybe that wouldn't be any better either.)

Q: Is it okay to say to someone recently told they are going to die, "Hey, you look pretty good for a dead guy!" (Yep, this was said to us.)
A: Nope.

Q: Is it acceptable to say to a spouse or partner of someone dying, someone younger, perhaps in their 30s or 40s, "You're still young. You'll bounce back. Just think how I would feel if (insert spouse's name here) died. We've been married for nearly 50 years!"
A: No. Do you know how lucky you are? Isn't that what we all hope for when we marry? When we make a lifelong commitment to the person we love—that we have the chance, the opportunity to live a long and healthy life with one another, to grow old with our spouse? To be blessed with that gift, the decades together with a beloved life partner? Well, that's as good as it gets. I always wanted to say, "How lucky you are. I didn't get that chance, to grow old with John. I would have given anything for that opportunity." Bounce back? Who knows?

I suppose so — that sometimes annoying resilience thing. But, again, all of us should be so fortunate to have that one special person, the one we choose above all others to spend our lives with — aged and together, still. To lose it early on is not a blessing, is not a better fate. I got short-changed.

Q: Is it okay, maybe comic relief, to mimic a dying friend's crippling side effects or symptoms, say, by talking in a breathy, labored, barely audible voice, or walking hunched over like a cripple and wobbling around with an imaginary cane?

A: No. This one I don't have a response for, nor did John and I during the two unfortunate occasions. The only comment I'll offer is a head shake.

Q: Is it all right, not seen as overly simplistic, to say to a loved one who has found out they are dying, "I don't know what to say." Or just, "I'm so sorry"?

A: Yes! Sometimes, less is more. Those words can be profound, heartfelt, and comforting to those going through the crisis. Don't attempt to fight your way through a tangle of words when you don't know what to say. Inevitably, you'll knot yourself up in ways you cannot imagine, and later kick yourself for it if you've managed to untangle yourself! Nobody knows what to say when they first hear of a loved one's diagnosis. Saying that you don't is straightforward and honest. That is what is important. "I am sorry" speaks volumes. Just stop there. The rest is better left unsaid.

The above primer is not meant to be mean spirited but rather, tongue in cheek. Although, at the time these things were said to us, they were anything but amusing, and they stung. The passage of time, however, offers a unique perspective. All of the above comments and physical "comic relief" were expressed by loving, compassionate, and intelligent friends. We all slip up. I do. If we would just take a moment to stop, breathe, think, and assess, we might make better choices in the words we offer to those who are enduring a crisis we cannot begin to comprehend in its complexity, and how very fragile their emotional psyches may be at that time.

CHAPTER 26

Welcome to the Club
(whether you like it or not)

*On the plus side, death is one of the few things
that can be done as easily lying down.*

~ Woody Allen

It was Groucho Marx who said, "I don't want to belong to any club that would have me as a member." I know what he meant.

It was not by choice that I became a card-carrying member of the Widow's Club. Most of the time, the decision is not yours to make. It's an odd club to be a part of—you don't join, sign membership papers, pay dues, meet for Bingo. Suddenly, you are just there; part of this invisible, floating entity that means nothing, and everything. Although it is intangible, this club, there is nothing nebulous about its membership. It is rather strict, really. Rules will be rules. You cannot join by pledging dollars or clipping coupons, by running fast or making the best three-bean salad. The upside, on the other hand, is that it's an equal opportunity club. It does not discriminate. Young, old, fat, thin, black, white, rich, poor. We can all become part of the club if we have one thing in common: death. The loss of a husband. I was handed my lifelong membership early on, at 43. While there are many members even younger, for the most part the inductees are usually elderly. It does make one feel a bit out of place. Like Groucho, I would like to offer my resignation, but this is one club where you cannot slip out the back door.

We love to put labels on things, on people. Already, and before the club, I had too many labels: Caucasian, heterosexual, woman, daughter, sister, aunt, friend, Californian, writer, wife, childless, caregiver, middle aged. Now I get to add "widow." Maybe if I can scratch off one more label, I'll win a prize.

As much as I do not care for this new label, I do find I get irritated when certain forms or documents don't take this membership into account. Many forms say "Check one only — single/married/divorced." They need to know why someone is single, but only if it is by divorce. They do not want to know if one is single due to death. This is more information than they need, or want. They'll take your age, height, weight, hair, and eye color. Maybe even ask for distinguishing marks, such as tattoos or moles or unsightly scars. But are you widowed? Uh, uh. That is way more than we want to know. Death is not something we like to acknowledge — even if only by checking a box.

With all my complaining about the Widow's Club, I feel bad for the few who would have liked membership but were denied. In some strange, twisted way, saying you are a widow may offer "benefits" that would otherwise be denied to someone not married but had nonetheless lost a partner. I use the term "benefits" loosely, as offhand, I can think of none other than the $255 "death benefit" offered to a widow/widower through Social Security. I prefer to call it the "death insult" — a few hundred bucks doesn't help much when you've lost a spouse, but it did pay for the libation at John's wake.

Seriously though, for those who are unmarried, or denied the legality of marriage and lose a life partner, I do know that there may be some comfort, or weight, in being able to say, "I am widowed. I lost my husband (or wife)." Even on those "Don't ask, don't tell" forms, being able to check "widowed" might make a small difference, an acknowledgment perhaps, that their loss was just as great, just as difficult. Sadly, we tend to give more credence or legitimacy to someone who has lost a "legal" partner as opposed to those who didn't or couldn't sign the paperwork, didn't check all the appropriate boxes. Unfair, I think. Love is love. Loss is loss. All profound and life changing. And, inevitably, for all of us, the outcome is the same. It is then, and especially then, when a piece of paper makes no difference at all.

Therefore, after careful evaluation, I guess the Widow's Club does discriminate. It denies membership to those without the legal paperwork.

On these grounds, I insist that the Widow's Club accept my resignation — or at least offer Bingo and a wine bar.

"Nice try."

CHAPTER 27

A Pocketful of Ashes

*A man's dying is more the
survivor's affair than his own.*

~ Thomas Mann

I began the great adventure with my family, husband John, and our two cats, Leo and Petunia. They were like our children, and they gave us great joy. Together, we embarked on the long journey from San Francisco to the windswept shores of Maine. Here, we created a new home, the four us. We had planned to live here, together, for a very long time. We were quite fortunate then.

Now, I am alone. Left alone — outliving them all, my family. Alone, I have lived through the struggles and deaths of the three lives that were the most meaningful to me; gave me the greatest happiness, abundant laughter, a sense of peace. That is what family is. They round you out. They give you greater purpose, make you complete. They make you whole. Then, I was a whole lot of whole.

In this big house, now, house-not-home, I live with three small boxes. Boxes of ash. John. Leo. Petunia. I have survived all of the life and love I moved with to Maine. My anchors, my richness, my heartbeat. All that life and energy, all that joy. Gone.

While I remain the same, they are now small. I can fit my family in my pocket. A pocket-sized family. A pocketful of ashes. Soon, I will mix them as one. Then, instead of three small family members in three small boxes, I will have one bigger box. A larger family of remains, lumped as one into my pocket. I suppose I'll need a bigger pocket. It's a good thing I didn't keep the ashes of my father and grandparents. I would have needed special-order pockets made, extra large, and that could have been costly.

They will go with me, wherever I go. Wherever that is. Today, I have no idea where I will make my home, or when. I will leave Maine, the place where I lived with my family, once. Oh! The entire universe, and no place to go. No place home. No sense of home. Homeless.

From now on, all my clothes will have to sport pockets. Pockets for my traveling family. Maybe I can join the circus. "See the lady whose tiny family fits in her pocket!" I'll definitely need pockets. So they can always be with me, wherever I go. Wherever that is.

PART III

The Next Journey

Kenya ~ 2003

*There were so many things. There were dik-dik and
leopard, kongoni and warthog, buffalo, lion, and the hare
that jumps — And there were wildebeest and antelope.
There was the snake that crawls and the snake that climbs.
There were birds, and young men like whips of leather,
like rainshafts in the sun, like spears before a singiri.
"Amut yut!" the young men would say,
"Here! Bend down and look. Bend down and
look at this mark. See how the leaf is crushed —
Bend down and look so that you may learn!"
And so, in time, I learned. But some
things I learned alone.*

~ Beryl Markham, *West With The Night*

CHAPTER 28

A Promise Kept

"Hope" is the thing with feathers —
That perches in the soul —
And sings the tune without the words —
And never stops — at all —

~ Emily Dickinson

Before he died, one of the last things John whispered to me was, "Go back to Africa. Keep writing. Be happy again." Better than anyone, he knew of the powerful grip that Africa had on me, the spiritual connection I felt with the continent, and how happy, fulfilled, and at peace I was when on her soil. During the years of his illness and following his death, not a day went by when my mind didn't return there. I longed for Africa each morning and took her dreams with me to bed each night. Perhaps more than anything, the determination and hope of someday returning sustained me throughout the most difficult moments. And there were many.

My first trip to Africa was with John in 1998. Along with two friends, we spent a glorious five weeks in South Africa. John was sick then, how ill we did not yet know. But, secretly, my gut told me he was terminal, and I suppose I knew then that, with John, I would never return to Africa. Toward the end of our trip, John's energy waning, we spent an easy day exploring shops and museums around Durban. We slipped into a small bookshop and went our separate ways. John was looking for a book by Bosman; I was looking for something, anything, about Africa. The proprietor asked if he could help me find a book. I told him I wanted a nonfiction book about Africa. Without hesitation, he said, "I think I know the book you'd like." He led me to a table toward the back of the shop that held a few copies of *I Dreamed of Africa* by Kuki Gallmann. "I think you should read this book," he said. He seemed very convincing, but I was surprised that he was determined to sell me a book about Kenya. There were many books in his shop on South Africa, one of which I assumed he would recommend. Since he was so convinced I should read her book, I bought it.

That night, as John and our friends went out to dinner, I stayed back at the hotel and read. I finished her book in the early hours of the morning. Before that afternoon, I had never heard of Kuki Gallmann or her bestselling book. Not only was it an amazing story and beautifully written, it was about the resilience of a woman who tragically lost her husband in Kenya some years earlier, and while still in her 30s. Just a short time later, she lost her only son as well. I too was in my 30s and facing the possibility of losing John, although at that time, we were not sure what was ailing him, ALS had been mentioned, but so had many other diseases. It was still early on and a definitive diagnosis had yet to be made. The book hit me hard. There were many similarities between this woman and me, primarily our passion for Africa. Born in Italy, and now living in Kenya, Gallmann's love affair with Africa began in childhood, as did mine. Following the death of her husband and son, she founded the Gallmann Memorial Foundation, creating a protected wildlife refuge, a science/research facility, and the Wilderness School on her 100,000 acres, Ol ari Nyiro, in remote northern Kenya. At that moment, my hope took a different turn. Not only would I see John through whatever was plaguing his body, but, no matter what unfolded and what hand fate would deal, Africa would play a major role in my life.

When we returned to the States, I emailed Kuki Gallmann in Kenya. I told her how much hope her book had given me, about

John's illness, and how I longed to see East Africa someday. Over the next few years, we corresponded via email and post. By then, John's diagnosis became terminal — ALS, a fate we hoped against all odds was not the one we would be dealt. All along, in her emails, Kuki wrote, "Come back to Africa, to Kenya. It is a healing place." I knew it would be; it was just a matter of how long it would take me to get back, to begin to heal. John and I began sending boxes full of books to the Gallmann Memorial Foundation. The books were used at her school for children, in memory of her son, as well as in the local library on her reserve. We tried to play a small role, in any way we could, which included my writing grant proposals to the Bushnell Corporation, which garnered the generous donation of a dozen pair of high-powered, night-vision binoculars for the anti-poaching patrol on Kuki's wildlife reserve. While our involvement was minor, it made both John and me feel as though we were doing our small part for Africa, together, even if we could not be there.

After publishing a travel article about South Africa for *The New York Times* in early 1999, I was contacted by Conservation Corporation Africa and extended an invitation to visit any two of their world-renowned safari camps in Africa. It was an unexpected and unbelievably generous offer. While John's health was deteriorating, he was still upright, albeit using a walker, and somewhat strong, and he was determined that I go back to Africa. As he would tell me repeatedly while I agonized over the thought of leaving him, "I'll be okay. This is a chance of a lifetime. You have to go." With the nudging and reassurances from our family doctor, Elizabeth Weiss, that John would be okay if I left him for three weeks, and under the care of his sister (formerly a nurse) who graciously agreed to fly from her home in Hawaii to look after him, I decided to go.

Along with a friend from San Francisco, we flew to Kenya and spent over three glorious weeks at the major wildlife reserves—from the red dust of Tsavo, to the great plains of elephant herds of Amboseli with its magnificent backdrop of snow-capped Kilimanjaro, the Aberdares, to the arid Samburu reserve on the northern fringes of the country. We saw thousands of shimmering, pink flamingos, flitting across the alkaline waters of Lake Nakuru; visited the Jane Goodall Sweetwaters Chimpanzee Sanctuary at Ol Pejeta Conservancy near Mount Kenya; and ended with an extraordinary stay at the Conservation Corps camp, Kichwa Bateleur, in the legendary Masai Mara. On our last night at Kichwa, our evening meal was set out amidst the plains. Tables were dressed in crisp, white linen and set with sparkling china and crystal. Around the camp, glowing brass lanterns cast dancing shadows across the grasses. While meats roasted on open flames, and coaxed by the gracious Masai employees, we joined them in song and dance around a blazing fire, as lions roared in the not-so-far distance. It was indeed a chance of a lifetime. It renewed my spirit and strength for the battle that was yet to come and would consume both John and me for the next two years. I did not know it then, but for those next two years, I would not travel beyond a 15-mile radius of our home as a full-time caregiver.

The last night in Kenya, I got a call in my hotel room in Nairobi. Kuki Gallmann's assistant was on the line, hoping that we could fly to Ol ari Nyiro the next day to meet Kuki. I had tried unsuccessfully to notify her before my trip, but, as she was out of the country, the correspondence never reached her. We were not to meet on that trip. It would be another three years, and I would be a new widow by the time our paths would cross.

Shortly after John's death, I emailed Kuki of his passing. Her offer still held: Come back to Kenya to heal, to Ol ari Nyiro. When I was able, I planned my month-long solo trip back to Africa. With John's and my combined frequent-flyer miles, I booked my roundtrip flight from Boston via London and onto Nairobi. I planned on staying the majority of my time at Kuki's science and research camp, a few days following at her beautiful tented camp, Makena's Hills (a special gift I was to give myself on the occasion of my birthday), then onto Olerai House, on the fertile banks of Lake Naivasha. All was going according to plan. The catch was that the United States was now at war in Iraq and, with terrorism phobia running rampant, the U.S. State Department issued a warning of imminent danger in Kenya, a probable terrorist bombing attack in Nairobi. For the first time in their history, British Airways suspended all flights into Nairobi. My flight.

Once again, my life was on hold. All along, I was determined to get there. The plan became to fly from London to Entebbe, Uganda, on British Airways, then take a charter flight to Nairobi. I was willing to go this extended route, ignore the State Department warnings, and get to Kenya on what would be just over one year following John's death. For weeks, I did not know for sure how my plans would unfold, as British Airways continued to change or modify flight plans. Just as I contemplated canceling the trip, on the morning of June 27, 2003—exactly one year to the day of John's passing—British Airways lifted its month-old ban of flying into Nairobi. That was the only signal I needed to make this solo journey.

"Go back to Africa. Be happy again."

I was on my way. Everything went without a hitch. It was both liberating and empowering to make such a trip on my own, to give myself the greatest gift I could have imagined: the gift of Africa. I had hoped to meet interesting people from around the world both at the science/research center at Kuki's reserve in the Laikipia region of northern Kenya, as well as at Olerai House located on beautiful Lake Naivasha. However, due to the perceived terrorist threats and supposed imminent danger, those who had scheduled time at the reserve and at Lake Naivasha had canceled. In more ways than I could have imagined, being the only guest wherever I went afforded me the greatest opportunities and newfound friendships. I met, got to know, and spent quality time with the employees — wonderful Kenyans who offered me so much. My lessons learned were invaluable; the friendships made, real and lasting. I am a better person for their friendship. I will forever be grateful.

I met with Kuki on several occasions, and our talks were honest and healing in myriad ways. Those who worked on the reserve, and in many capacities, were giving and helpful to a fault. The connections I made there, specifically with those at the science and research camp, were some of the deepest and most introspective of my life. Jeffrey Muchugi, my main guide while at the camp, a brilliant mind and human being who taught me so much about the bush, both flora and fauna. We spent hours talking and trekking in the bush, discussing politics, family, friends, world issues, the environment, books, and life. We joked, easily. Douglas Nagi, the top guide at Kuki's reserve ("the walking encyclopedia," as they call him), a thoughtful, intelligent, straightforward man whose candid conversation and love for the wild brought a richness to my days. Philip Ochieng, the resident entomologist, who always had a smile on his face and got giddy at the sight of or talking about lovely things with wings—butterflies, lacewings, insects, and moths. It was Philip, who, on my birthday, asked if I would make him a small cake for afternoon tea. I had baked a cake for the staff the day before, and Philip had liked it so much that it didn't matter what day it was. He just laughed and asked if I didn't mind; I didn't. And Jones, the multitask man for Kuki, whom I spent some time talking with at Makena's Hills. A shy, dear, soft-spoken man who made me feel as though I were at home. One afternoon while I was out walking, Jones, in all seriousness, came up to me and, in a quiet, fatherly voice, said, "You need to eat something. You look thin." And *Mzee* Epateti, the tracker, *askari* (guard), and retired Kenyan Wildlife Service ranger, who led my foot safaris and kept me safe. He loved the bush, as do I, and he taught me much. The bush was a part of him. He was the bush. So many more, as well—from the fabulous cook, *Mzee* Christopher, who generously allowed me to rummage through his kitchen sanctuary to bake cakes (far inferior to his own); to Elizabeth, and Ali. These remarkable individuals brought joy into my life once again. They took great care of me at a time when I could not have appreciated more the chance and opportunity to be cared for. For the first time in many, many months, I did not feel so alone.

Asante Sana.

CHAPTER 29

Science/Research Camp at Ol ari Nyiro

*In all things of nature there
is something of the marvelous.*

~ Aristotle

After a pot of Kenyan coffee and fresh melon, I move a wicker chair to the grass and garden area to watch birds, write, and reflect. I have been here for three days now, with my solitude. Other than two young volunteers, there are no other visitors. The camp stands empty, the row of tents that would otherwise house researchers and scientists from around the globe sit still and silent.

A lizard is sunning itself on a tiered ledge in a small, ornamental rock garden. He has managed to find the single ray of sun that has fingered its way through a cloud-filled sky. He is lying there now, watching me write, watching me watching it. Finally, it relaxes in its warm sunbath and, for a moment, closes its eyes.

The sky is filling with dark, ominous clouds as it seems to do most early afternoons, threatening rain. This is the dry season, but rain has been plentiful these days. The garden is relishing the unexpected moisture and is resplendent with bougainvillea, poinsettia, jasmine, euphorbia and fever trees, formidable succulents, draping vines, and myriad wildflowers.

From where I sit and write, I look onto a landscape and horizon I had only dreamed about in some small way, in my imagination. Across the expanse of grass, the fever trees and euphorbia, the Great Rift Valley, a wave of ancient mountains and plateaus seemingly go on forever. The African sky, more vast and changeable than words can describe or past experience can compare, is blue and clear; then, at once, filled with enormous, billowing clouds of different shapes and tones, from brilliant white to metal gray. The clouds create fast-moving pockets of light and shadow across this ancient landscape, invoking varied moods and thoughts. All around me, light changes, warm sun turns to a cold breeze, unexpected raindrops against my skin, then back to a dry, burning sun.

CHAPTER 30

It Is Always Good to Be Afraid of Something

All nature wears one universal grin.

~ Henry Fielding

The night was long. Admittedly, though frightened at times, I was more excited over the commotion outside my cottage. This rustic, single-room cottage, one of two at the research center, is a solid structure with a thatched roof. Where walls would normally meet the ceiling, however, it is "open" except for chicken wire, which runs along the perimeter of the room and is about 1 foot high. The bathroom is located outside my room, a few steps from my door. But, by night, it feels like a very long way. Bats, last night, were quite active—inside my room. I suppose, due to the chicken-wire construction, bugs and assorted insects are as easy a catch inside the room as they are outside. The bats were noisy, though, and at times actually hit the mosquito net surrounding my bed. I was glad I had the foresight to tuck the netting between the mattresses—more as a paranoid precaution for things that crawl or slither. I have always heard that bats have an incredible sense of radar. Not necessarily so with these bats. Besides smacking into the bedding, I heard a few ram into the wood furniture, which was equally disconcerting. And then there was the guano, next morning, speckled about my shoes and toiletries, which I really didn't mind so much.

The night, however, was not long because of the bat ruckus and thoughts of impending guano. It was the animal commotion outside my room. Naturally, just as my bladder decided to fill beyond capacity, hyena decided to inspect the camp, and my cottage seemed to be of some particular interest. There is no mistaking the vocalizations of the hyena. I do love their sounds, most of the time, but not when I have to pee, and it's dark, and I have to leave my room with nothing between me and the hyena but a kerosene lamp. I know it is a safe journey to make. Hyena are basically scavengers and don't attack. But I do remember hearing, on a previous trip to Kenya, that two hyena had attacked an employee at a tented camp in the Masai Mara game reserve. My bladder, as it often does, wins out and, with lantern in tow, I brave the few steps to the toilet.

It seems to be a rotating visit of the wild, and, not long after my return to bed, elephants arrive. Evidently, the fresh, succulent produce from the nearby kitchen garden is irresistible, not to mention the inviting smorgasbord of euphorbia, aloe, and fragrant flowers growing outside my windows. One loses stature when in the company of elephants. You shrink, in all manners, dwarfed both literally and figuratively. It is easy to find humility when in the presence of these massive and wonderful creatures. Easily, an adult elephant will stand higher than my thatched ceiling and, knowing that a family munches just a few feet away, is the very definition of humbling. I love the sounds of their low, calibrated breathing; the deep, guttural rumblings of their stomachs. I could hear every breath, munch, chew, rumble, and passage of gas that night—outside my room. And, when they finally had enough, had eaten a goodly portion of the garden produce meant for the employees and visitors, they ambled into the night, leaving way for the next visitors, now early morning, a small pride of lions. Just before daybreak, I hear their muffled grunts and roars. They are near the main camp, and I was told that, just a few days earlier, they had been feasting on a zebra kill on the grounds of the tented research camp not that far from my room.

The following afternoon, just before dusk, Jeffrey and Epateti take me for a short game drive. We cover quite a bit of ground, but there are very few animals in sight, which Jeffrey attributes to an impending storm. Just as we decide to head back, a small family of four elephants emerges from a cluster of dense bush on an otherwise open plain. There is one adult, two subadults, and one newborn calf, which Jeffrey and Epateti determine to be all of one month old. The tiny family was well hidden in this cluster, and we had not seen it, nor had they heard our approach.

Frightened, the oldest and largest of the group emerges, agitated and protective of her newborn as only an elephant mother can be. We are equally as startled, but the elephant is especially upset with our intrusion and trumpets loudly. Ears outstretched in an attempt to look even larger than she already is, she moves quickly toward the vehicle. While elephants are slow walkers, amblers, they can move rapidly when fleeing or charging, and Epateti is fully aware of her agitation. He steps on the gas just as Jeffrey yells, "Move!" and the mother elephant begins to gain ground on the old, rusty jeep. Had we been on foot, this would have been a very serious matter, as elephants can charge at speeds topping 25 miles per hour, far faster than a human can run. Fortunately, in the vehicle, we are able to pull away and allow the family the space they need to once again feel secure. I am told that the elephant's reaction was a bit extreme and, had we not surprised them and if a calf had not been present, the mother elephant more than likely would not have displayed such aggression. I have a deep respect for elephants. You do as they dictate.

As we drive across the open plain, the sky becomes increasingly ominous, turning steely gray to black. Jeffrey sees the storm approaching and tells Epateti that we must make good time in getting back to camp. I sense Epateti knows this, as his foot is already heavy on the pedal. For miles around, there is nothing more than dry, open ground and an endless, threatening sky. On the horizon, I watch as bolts of lightning strike the earth, violent streaks of light shattering across the desolate landscape. For whatever reason, lightning is my biggest fear, my phobia. As Jeffrey and I stand in the jeep, the roof open to the heavens and approaching storm, and as the blackened sky continues to flash, I tell Jeffrey of my fear of lightning. At this moment, I am scared, aware of our vulnerability on the open plains; aware of the rusting, metal vehicle in which I am riding. As the bolts crash all around, Jeffrey pats my arm and says, "It is okay, Jan, to be afraid of lightning. I don't like lightning either. It is always good to be afraid of something."

His words calm me. His acknowledgment that he too is at times afraid of lightning—more important, that he acknowledged and respected my fear—makes me somehow less frightened. I watch the bolts continue to rip and tear across the landscape. I smile, thinking all the while that it was reminiscent of a scene out of a *National Geographic* special on violent African storms. Here I was, in the middle of a lightning storm in the middle of the African bush, no one around for miles, in a metal jeep. It seemed appropriate. And, if I was going to be hit by lightning, damn it, I couldn't think of a place I'd rather be.

CHAPTER 31

Tracking an Injured Elephant

In wildness is the preservation of the world.

~ Thoreau

After lunch with Philip, the resident entomologist at the science/research center, I am asked if I would like to join him and a few others in tracking a wounded elephant on the reserve. "We must hurry," Philip says, moving toward the awaiting vehicle. "Time is of the essence." I jump in, Epateti at the wheel, with a handful of guards, trackers, and rangers crammed into the jeep. Everyone is speaking hurriedly, excitedly, about an elephant feared injured by the spear of a local farmer. We drive to the perimeter of the reserve and, along the fence line, two awaiting *askaris* (guards) show us faint elephant tracks dotted with blood. It appears the elephant had gotten over the perimeter boundary fence and onto private land, more than likely eating the crops on a neighboring farm or farms. The animal was pursued by a farmer, speared, then chased back onto the grounds of Ol ari Nyiro, wounded and bleeding.

Spearing an elephant is serious business. It is illegal, as they are an endangered species and deemed protected wildlife. If caught, the accused could face up to 15 years in prison. It's a horrible fate when an elephant is speared. The animal dies a slow and painful death and suffers greatly, as the tip of the weapon is coated with a deadly poison. It's not uncommon in these parts—man and elephant have always been at odds. The elephant habitat continues to be compromised, diminishing due to human encroachment, and the survival of the elephant means that food must be found, wherever it happens to be. An elephant does not know boundaries. In contrast, the very existence of a farmer is his crops, and an elephant or herd can wipe out a single crop, a livelihood, threatening the farmer's survival. It is a conflict seemingly without solution and, sadly, lives of both warring species are lost.

For many hours, over the fence line of the reserve and onto neighboring land toward the *manyatta* (village) of Ol Moran, I follow the expert trackers along the scene of the crime. Indiscernible to the untrained eye, I can barely detect the tracks left by the farmer. And yet, to the trackers, they are quite clear and tell a vivid and detailed story. After some time investigating in the dense scrub, the trackers find a promising clue: sandal prints surrounded by areas of broken twigs and disturbed earth. It is the spot where man and animal fought, where the doomed elephant took a spear to its flesh.

One tracker snaps a long twig from a leleshwa bush and measures the length of the sandal print. Cutting the twig to size, he measures it against his own foot and determines the shoe size of the farmer. While the trackers have determined the location of the attack scene, Epateti drives to the village to speak with the Turkana chief, asking him to join us where the apparent spearing took place. An hour or so later, Epateti arrives with the chief, who greets all of us with a firm handshake. He is shown the spot where the altercation took place, the sandal prints, the broken twigs, depressions and marks in the dry soil where farmer and elephant collided. It is the chief's duty to investigate and find out who has injured the elephant. Fact is, however, many of the local farmers have gone uncaught after past spearings, and fellow villagers are reluctant to offer any information leading to the arrest of a farmer who has illegally speared an elephant. While the effort in tracking down those who harm or kill endangered wildlife might seem futile, it is the law, and necessary protocol must be followed as the numbers of these magnificent animals — elephants — continue to dwindle.

As daylight fades, we drive the chief back to his *manyatta* of Ol Moran. This is Epateti's village too and, as the jeep comes to a halt, he is greeted by many friends and family. I am up front with Epateti, and the villagers greet me as well — smiling, offering handshakes, children waving and giggling. The *manyatta* is unlike anything I've seen. Seemingly poverty stricken, it is comprised of mainly Turkana and Samburu, but there are a few Pokots and other ethnic groups as well. Emaciated dogs, goats, and chickens scramble across the dusty dirt paths. Buildings are tiny, earthen huts; thatched roofs or loose metal sheets atop the structures, which have few or no windows and barely look as if they can withstand the very weight of their tops. There is a handful of stores: tiny, dark rooms offering little from what I can see from my seat. It is hard to imagine that anyone lives here, let alone survives. But they do.

All around me, everyone is smiling. Why do they appear so happy? Why does everyone, especially the children, show so much heartfelt affection toward me, in greeting me with warm handshakes and even warmer smiles? Is it because of their deep affection for Epateti and the fact that I am sitting beside him? Am I graciously afforded this outpouring of kindness due to nothing more than my proximity to someone they care for who is important to them?

I view a poor village scene that appears so very limited, seems to offer little hope. And, yet, is it not my view as well that is limited? Are my visions not small and contained in light of a bigger picture? We know what we know. And what we have is what we know. I have infinitely more in terms of creature comforts, in a world of overabundance. Their world is based on community, family and friends, and the land. Perhaps what they lack in creature comforts they make up for in community spirit, a survival based on togetherness, cooperation, and extended hospitality. It is a balance that is missing — in both worlds.

The last thing I see as we pull away from the *manyatta* is a weathered sign above the door of the local pub. The pub is nearly dark, but the last of the daylight illuminates the placard — an ad for Tusker beer, a sign showing the head of a regal elephant with long, massive tusks.

I do not know the fate of the villager who speared the elephant. The fate of the elephant, however, is not as ambiguous.

CHAPTER 32

Same Sun and Moon (for Epateti)

Thou were my guide, philosopher, and friend.

~ Alexander Pope

After breakfast, Jeffrey and I prepare for a bushwalk. Jeffrey, my guide while at the science/research camp, and the *askari* (guard), Epateti, will take me for my first safari on foot. This is my third trip to Africa, second to Kenya, and I have only witnessed the bush, the wild, from Land Rover or jeep. I am beyond excited—both exhilarated and frightened.

Epateti is a retired ranger and antipoaching guard for the Kenyan Wildlife Service (KWS). He worked for them for nearly 40 years, training as a young boy. I say "young boy," but they age differently here, in Africa. By age 12 or so, a boy may be considered more man than boy, and responsibilities are often much greater than what one experiences in the States. Epateti had killed 15 poachers during his time with the KWS, and some of those killed had not only poached wildlife but had attempted or killed KWS rangers as well.

Epateti has a wonderful smile. His skin is dark, like black coffee, and the whites of his eyes are the color of weak tea. When he smiles, his eyes shine. He is lean and wiry. He is an older Turkana. I don't know his age, but he looks very old to me. Initially I wonder if someone "this old" is capable of guiding me through the bush, protecting me from possible danger. After all, I'll be on foot, on equal ground with elephant, buffalo, and lion. But that concern quickly fades as I realize that he would not be in charge of this safari if not extremely capable and respected. Forty years with the KWS have honed his senses of the bush, of everything wild, and like no one else. I am told he should be addressed as *Mzee* Epateti. *Mzee* roughly means "old man" but is truly an address of respect. Unlike many Americans, Africans have great respect for their elders.

Jeffrey, a highly experienced Bronze Medal Guide, does all the translating between Epateti and me. Jeffrey and Epateti communicate in Kiswahili. I am told that if we are encountered—especially by an aggressive, lone male buffalo—not to make a sound, not to run, but to quickly scout out my surroundings, and then, fast, drop to the ground! More times than not, I am told not to run, dependent upon what animal poses threat. I understand this. I know that, if I run, I will be chased. I will be seen as prey. But how does one turn off instinct coupled with adrenaline (not to mention abject fear!) and stay put, dropping flat to the ground? I hope I don't have the opportunity to find out. Epateti will always be in the lead with his expert knowledge of the bush and rifle; Jeffrey will be close behind; I will follow, even closer.

These two men, strangers to me, are leading me deep into the bush. I have signed an indemnity form, saying that I understand I'm in the wilds of Kenya and hold no responsibility toward the reserve/research center should anything happen to me. This is wild territory, the Laikipia region of northern Kenya, not a theme park. Accidents happen and, although rare, people are killed on this land. It is the way of life when you live in the bush. You share your home with the wild (better yet, the wild shares its home with you), and you learn to respect and appreciate what lives alongside you. So I am entrusting my safety to these men, these strangers until a few days ago. Oddly enough, I have rarely felt safer.

Both men are experts on spoor and, within minutes of our bushwalk, they spot fresh buffalo and elephant prints. These are two animals you don't necessarily want to disturb in the wild. A lone bull buffalo is extremely dangerous and alarmingly cunning, and elephants with baby or babies in tow do not tolerate close proximity. For all of their girth, they are fast and will run down a human in no time flat. There are only a few pockets of trees — mostly low, dense scrub, which provides excellent cover for myriad smaller animals. Epateti stops and points a long, weathered finger toward the dusty earth. A leopard has been tracking here, fairly recently, and, from the spoor just ahead of the leopard's, it appears to be tracking a baboon.

During the course of our bushwalk, I am educated on dung and spoor, blossoms, leaves, and bark. We eat wild berries along the way. I am shown plants that are used as natural insect repellents for animals, made into chai tea, and used as an antimalarial remedy by the Turkana. While Jeffrey tells me about this plant, Epateti suddenly motions to halt and be silent. He has spotted fresh buffalo spoor followed by a flock of alarmed oxpecker birds taking flight. He points to a dense clump of bush ahead. Hidden in the thicket, a buffalo lurks. This is not a spot to linger. Quietly and on guard, we leave the area.

It's surprisingly hot this afternoon. Following a cool, damp morning, the sun, after hiding behind dense cloud cover, has pushed through hotter and brighter than expected. This stretch of bush has gotten flatter and more arid, the ground parched and dry. Epateti stops, looks skyward, and squints toward the sun. He is animated and smiling broadly. He is talking rapidly to Jeffrey, to the sky, hands motioning to the sun, grinning and shaking his head. "What is he saying?" I ask. "Ah, ah," Jeffrey nods. "Epateti is amazed," he says, "that the same sun overhead now, this very sun, and the same sun with him every day, is the very same sun that you see and feel in America, many oceans away." Epateti smiles, his eyes dancing, while Jeffrey translates his words. These words and his excitement seem to have stemmed from a profound wonderment and appreciation of life, the planet, the universe, a higher spirit, all evident on his expressive face. Suddenly, the dark, wrinkled face that looked so old and worn to me just hours before appears young and smooth and vibrant. I smile at Epateti and ask Jeffrey to translate. "Please tell him that I am often amazed by the same thing. Just before I left for Kenya, I stood on my deck in Maine one evening, gazed up at a full moon, and thought to myself, "This is the very same moon being gazed upon by people in Africa." Epateti nods and laughs, walking forward in the dust and sun, with his rifle, leading.

The three hours on foot pass quickly. We have covered over 15 miles under a relentless midday sun; tired, we head back to camp. At the center, exhausted and sunburned, I join Jeffrey for a lunch of homemade samosas and pizza, fresh green beans and salad from the organic garden, and large, juicy slices of melon.

Next morning, I rise early after a fairly decent sleep. Only the sounds of distant lions, a few hyenas roaming the camp, and snorting buffalo near my cottage had disturbed my otherwise peaceful sleep. Today, Jeffrey and I prepare for my second and more ambitious bushwalk. We join a smiling Epateti and, once again, head into the wild. Jeffrey warns that this safari will lead much deeper into the bush than before, and we must remain extremely quiet and vigilant. The area we will trek today has a denser animal population and yields more abundant vegetation for animals to hide behind or within. With Epateti upfront, we head into the deep thicket of thorn and scrub. We say little; pointing or a hushed whisper is our means of communication. More buffalo and rhino prints, herds of impala, a handful of zebra, an occasional warthog and other smaller mammals become part of our journey. I am constantly on the lookout for snakes, and it serves me well to remember to look down from time to time. What can crawl or slither on the ground can be as lovely or as dangerous as what lies beside and above.

It is amazingly quiet in the bush. The dominant sounds are our breaths and the snapping of twigs and leaves beneath our weight. We are making way through deeper brush and bramble, and Jeffrey is kind enough to hold back the larger branches that block our path. Constantly, the landscape changes, some areas so thick with vegetation that it is more reflective of dense forest than bush or plain. Dark, smelling of damp, fecund earth, and soft underfoot, the forest pockets are suddenly a play of light and ominous shadow, darting through limbs, lurking behind trunks, then out again into full, bright sunlight and open ground—arid, cracked, and solid.

There is nothing on the Earth that can compare to being on foot in and at one with the wild. No barrier or safety net; no metal vehicle between you and what roams wild. Your senses become highly sensitive, acute; the heart pounds faster and louder; the initial fear of the unknown, of danger, unfolds into a deeper sense of trust and letting go. Like most things in life, you cannot control nature, what is wild. And, when you give in to that reality, put your faith not only in your guide and *askari* but also in something higher—the spirit of Africa, of nature—a lovely dichotomy of exhilaration and calm prevails, a spiritual connection to all living things.

As quickly as my sense of calm envelopes, a sudden crunch and reverberating rumble in nearby bush break the peaceful silence. Instantly, Epateti motions Jeffrey and me to move back—*FAST!* Do not run but move without wasting any time! Jeffrey grabs my arm and quietly pulls me back a few meters, closer to a bushy area for cover. If I were not already anxious, seeing Jeffrey's expression makes me all the more concerned. Noiselessly, Epateti backs up in our direction, moving away from the sounds. His gun is aimed and rigid should the massive elephant decide to charge. My heart racing, I await Epateti's signal to once again move forward. It is safe now. The elephant has moved on, back into the thick cover of bush. I am acutely aware that my surroundings offer little safety of cover. Where we stand, on this stretch of wild, there are few trees. Only low bush and scrub, wild sage, and a handful of fragile-looking trees that would snap like brittle twigs during an elephant charge. Silently, we move farther into the bush and again stop, move back, and stay still so as not to alarm the small elephant family browsing just a few meters away. The tiny herd consists of five adult members and one calf approximately two to three years old. We watch them watching us. They relax a bit, recognizing our presence, and continue to browse.

Not far ahead, Epateti grabs my hand and pulls me toward an opening in the earth. He has spotted a hyena den and, at that very moment, a large male hyena pokes its head from the hole. Perhaps he felt our footsteps, the rumblings of the earth, and instantly it scrambles from the hole and into the cover of thicket.

It's getting hotter, and the heat of the sun brings a sudden heaviness of odor to the air. Jeffrey and Epateti lead me to the remains of a young bull elephant, perhaps 12 or so years old. It has recently died of what appears to be natural causes. The carcass is nearly picked clean; only a few rib bones, the immense skull, and brain remnants are left. A single chunk of skin lies near a rib bone. It has been eaten by lion and hyena, then picked over by vultures and other scavengers. The few decomposing parts, along with liquid remains dampening the earth, reek of a putrid smell that is nearly unbearable.

We continue our trek above miles of the Great Rift Valley, upwards through dense brush and vast open spaces of tall, yellow savannah grasses — perfect hiding places for lion, leopard, and cheetah. These high points reveal a magnificent landscape, an unbroken tapestry of rolling hills and plains, shades of lush greens and pale golds. Epateti has been silent for some time. Now he would like to talk. As we rest along a ridgeline and silently marvel at the pristine beauty, he reveals a painful chapter of his life, through Jeffrey and to me.

Epateti has two wives and seven children. He is 52 years old. Both Jeffrey and I are surprised to hear that he is so young. He has endured much in those five decades, and it can be read across his worn face. Epateti lost an earlier family. His wife was murdered in their home around 1983, he says. His children too were killed by the bandits who stole the *manyatta's* (village) cattle and murdered other families as well. Nearly 40 years working with the KWS also took its toll, and he was shot numerous times during his duty with the antipoaching patrol. Epateti's life has been a difficult one — one of grief and hardship — words he does not use but are evident in his dark eyes and the deep crevices of his face. I nod that I understand and tell him how very sorry I am for the loss of his family. I tell him that I lost my husband too, just a year ago, and I know of the profound sadness. Epateti shakes his head and quietly offers, "*Pole, pole,*" which means, "I am sorry, very sorry." His words are heartfelt, and his kind face reveals an understanding that can only be shared in its true depth with another who has experienced a similar loss.

The sun is moving lower in the sky, and we have been on foot for hours now. Jeffrey's enthusiasm has not yet faded, and he is determined to continue my education of the bush. He tears off a small branch from a wild sage bush and gives it to me to use as a fly swatter. He tells me that the sage plant, wild leleshwa, is important for four things: the leaves are harvested for their rich, aromatic oils, and the rest of the plant is used for making bowls or for firewood as well as harvested for coal production. Much of the land on this reserve is covered with wild leleshwa, and I have had the pleasure of bathing in its fragrant, emerald-green oil. Next, I'm shown different wild flowers to chew on if I run out of water while in the bush. Then he snips a delicate, soft-blue flower and squeezes a small drop into the palm of my hand. The blossom yields a clear, oily liquid that is a natural eyedrop and lubricant. Epateti breaks off a different specimen that works as a potent laxative, while another nearby plant is used by locals to treat prostate cancer. Some berries are extremely poisonous if eaten unripe but when fully ripened are highly nutritious. I am surrounded by plants, trees, flowers, and berries that offer invaluable gifts in the forms of necessities for survival as well as natural remedies—a veritable pharmacy in the middle of the African bush.

We are nearing the end of our walking safari and, after five hours, we have covered more than 22 miles of dense bush and open plain. We are hot and tired and decide to take one last rest before heading back to camp. We sit beneath a thorn tree, offering dappled shade from the still-burning sun, and sip water from Jeffrey's canteen. Epateti talks about his days with the KWS and, for dramatic effect, rolls up a pant leg to reveal the scars and depressions in his leg from poachers' bullets. After his stories are told and bullet wounds revealed, Epateti offers one last gift. He sees something beneath a small tree and is very excited about the find. Do I want it? "It is a giant mushroom," Jeffrey tells me. We walk to a diminutive tree, offering shade to one gargantuan mushroom, a single fungus the size of a small parasol. Epateti is determined that I have this wonderful delicacy and, with some effort, pulls the giant mushroom from the dirt, shakes it off, and hands me the lovely gift. "Are you sure you don't want it?" Jeffrey translates for me: "You keep it, *Mzee* Epateti." But Epateti would not have it, insisting rather that I bring it back to camp and ask *Mzee* Christopher to prepare it for the evening dinner. "It is a good mushroom," he says, "a delicious mushroom." "*Asante sana, Mzee.*" (Thank you.) We head back, the prehistoric-like mushroom held above my head as a mini parasol and blocking the sun—a motion that Epateti finds very amusing. As usual, he smiles broadly, his eyes dancing at the sight of a mushroom umbrella.

Along with a handful of other delectable dishes, *Mzee* Christopher, the incredible cook at the research center, has prepared the mammoth mushroom with olive oil and garlic and a few secret herbs and spices. There is enough for the four of us at dinner, with leftovers. It is simply delicious, perhaps more so because it was a gift, handpicked in the wild by my friend, Epateti.

A common language does not necessarily mean a communication through words. Speaking the same language might mean a connection on a deeper level; a bond borne from something our minds do not fully comprehend but is understood through our hearts. When this happens, it is one of the greatest gifts of being human. Most of my communication with Epateti over my weeks at the research center had little to do with words. Oftentimes, we would say something in our different languages and, without understanding the words, we were somehow able to translate the feelings or essence of what we were trying to convey, enough to understand, to make a connection. We would nod, smile, listen, feel, and comprehend through different expressions — the burst of joy revealed in a smile or laugh, the profound sadness exposed from one's eyes, the waving of hands — simple gestures, all meaningful and silently understood. Sometimes, words can get in the way. There are people on this earth who bond for whatever reason — for every reason and for no reason at all. By simply being human, by our common losses and triumphs, by a shared exhilaration over a breathtakingly beautiful stretch of savannah or the head of a hyena protruding from a den, the generosity in the gift of a giant mushroom, or the shared heartbreak over the loss of loved ones, we are able to make a higher connection with someone who has "happened" in our lives.

I do believe in destiny. For whatever reason, our paths were meant to cross, however brief. Epateti made a lasting impression on me. I was humbled and honored to have met him, and this was translated for him on my last evening at the camp. I learned from Epateti, this total stranger. There were things we saw with like eyes; things we endured with similar resolve and resilience. He had asked that a photo be taken of the two of us. He is standing in his dark-green khakis, and we pose for the shot, new friends.

The last time I saw him, it was dark. A wood fire was burning in the sitting room, and a few kerosene lamps lit the outside of *Mzee* Christopher's kitchen. It was raining. Philip was there to translate our farewell. We hugged and shook hands. I thanked him for his generosity, for guiding me safely through the bush, for all I had learned. I told him he was a good and kind man. I wished him well, always. He nodded to me and, in Kiswahili to Philip and translated to me, he said, "I know I will see you again, God willing." And, as usual, he smiled.

When I returned to the States, I sent a few gifts to my new friends at Ol ari Nyiro's research center. I sent books and pens and bags of sweets. Epateti liked Life Savers. He had never tasted them before. On one of our bushwalks, he had been coughing a lot and said that his throat was dry from the heat and dust. I pulled a roll of Life Savers from my pocket and offered him one. He had never tasted anything so sweet, he told Jeffrey. They made him feel better, made his throat well. When I was home, I sent him a large bag filled with Life Savers.

It has been nearly two years since my solo trip to Kenya, to Ol ari Nyiro. I received an email the other day, saying that Epateti had passed away since my visit there. It had not been by the wild or by a poacher's bullet but by the ravages of disease. I was deeply saddened by the news. I wept for my friend, perhaps more so for myself, knowing I would not see him again. I pulled out the photos from my trip and looked at the ones taken with Epateti. I was surprised at how young he looked, not like the old man I initially saw — the wrinkled, worn face of a man much older than his years. I saw a young, vital man standing strong in his dark-green khakis. His black, coffee-colored skin looking smooth and vibrant. The wisdom in his eyes, speaking volumes — even in a photograph.

As you once said to me, my friend, "I know I will see you again, God willing." And I do see you, Epateti. Each time I look at the sun and moon.

CHAPTER 33

An Adventure in the Mukutan Gorge

Nothing would give up life: Even the
dirt kept breathing a small breath.

~ Theodore Roethke

The Mukutan Gorge looks like another country unto itself. From the low scrub and bush rises a splendid place of converging canyons, steep mountains, and tropical, jungle-like vegetation surrounding crystalline waterfalls, pools, and streams. Getting there is not easy and not necessarily for the faint of heart.

Trekking through high grasses and down riverine banks darkened by lush, tropical plants and trees, the light changes once again as filtered sun cuts through dense foliage, playing hide and seek in the cool shadows. Across moss-covered rocks and running water, through walls of dripping palm fronds and branches heavy with lichen, the safari continues through this moist and fertile world, offering no easy footpath or break in trees.

Today, I am hiking the gorge with Douglas and Jeffrey, Philip, two armed guards, and two young women—one American, one German, who are volunteering at the research center. Not knowing beforehand that this trip would offer opportunities to be on foot in the bush (previous safaris in Africa were mostly confined to Land Rovers and never into open, wild bush), I didn't pack hiking boots appropriate for serious treks like this into the wild. The young German volunteer, Katarina, graciously offered a second pair of boots she had packed, so today, I am lugging them along. If not for the boots, I could not have done this spectacular hike; unfortunately, the boots are at least a size 10 while I wear a size 6. Some four sizes too big and extremely heavy, I feel as though I am walking with bowling balls attached to my feet. They look like military-issue footwear and, with each step, my small feet, which feel even tinier housed in these cavernous vessels, are swimming about with every move, regardless of the pair of socks stuffed into each toe. This adventure promises to be a lot more challenging, if not far more precarious, due to my immense footwear and their weight, and the difficult terrain from scouring cliffs to crossing rivers. At this moment, my humor is intact, but my gut tells me things may change as the real physical challenges emerge.

Our first stop is the "small waterfall," a gorgeous spot and respite in full sun. As we stand alongside the transparent pool waters at the base of the fall, Douglas gingerly pulls a plant from the banks and tells me to chew on it. He does the same, as does Jeffrey, watching my reaction to the taste of the pungent, yellow bud. As I chew, my mouth begins to burn, followed by the numbing of my tongue and throat. Douglas tells me that this medicinal plant is widely used as a remedy for sore throats and mouth ulcers.

Leaving the gentle sounds of the waterfall behind, we encounter the first of many walls of rock. In front of me is a vertical slab of mountain, perhaps 20 feet high. The only way up is by grasping at tiny lips of stone ledge while finding the few spots where a foot can grip, then hoisting oneself up and onto the base of the rock wall. I watch as the guides scramble effortlessly up the wall face. Naturally, they have done it before. In fact, I am the only one here today who has not yet made the trek through the Mukutan Gorge, so I am at a definite disadvantage, not to mention my feet. I make many attempts but cannot seem to grasp enough exposed ledge to hold my weight while simultaneously finding a foot grip large enough to manage my loose and massive boots. Finally, after numerous unsuccessful attempts, Katarina, just below, gives me a strong boost and push, which gives me the momentum to pull myself up and onto the top of the cliff wall. I do believe she owed me that, considering my ankles are attached to an additional 10 pounds of leather while scaling cliffs and trekking through jungle.

The next hurdle of this higher plateau is a slippery river crossing. The fast-running waters of the river are deceptive and potentially dangerous if one isn't mindful. Where a small waterway crests at the river site, we must carefully move across wet, algae-covered rocks and then, grasping the stone face of the cliff, maneuver our way across a piece of log, a fallen tree, that has wedged itself between the cliff and the water spillway and acts as a bridge. This is a precarious spot at best, hugging the smooth, flat cliff face while balancing one foot in front of the other along the length of the log, maybe 25 feet long. The drop below is far enough to be dangerous, into fast-moving, murky waters and onto jagged rocks. I am told, the first of numerous times this trek, not to look down while crossing. I obey and am relieved when my boots and I make it across the damp expanse of log, over the drop, safe. What a pair.

I'm aware that I am smiling broadly. I am by far the oldest in this group. The others barely top 30. In fact, they are all in their 20s, with the exception I believe of Philip, who may be just 30. In any event, as I have just celebrated my 45th birthday while at the research camp, and am now officially a *mama* (the term of respect for an older tribal woman), I think I have held up pretty well.

Jokingly, when I told Philip the day I turned 45 that I guessed he would now have to address me as *Mama* Jan, he giggled, good-naturedly. Actually, he laughed for some time.

The paradise of the Mukutan Gorge is similar to being transported into the tangles and depth of primordial jungle. It's a breathtaking spot, very different from the areas I've trekked the past few days — through savannah and vast, open plains; dry bush, thorn, and scrub. I have always dreamed about hiking the jungle, but the adventure to come will surely test my will and endurance.

For some reason, I assume that the most vigorous and challenging of cliff scaling is behind me. But, as we continue the safari, our single-file line of bodies — moving through wet foliage; over steep drops, raging waters, and chalky cliffs — a more ominous wall of rock looms ahead. This cliff, which offers no advantage of protruding ledge or lip to grasp, is higher than the last and has a far more frightening drop. I watch as a few of the others struggle, slowly, little by little, making their way along the face and to the other side. It is not so much climbing this wall that must be done as it's holding onto or grasping a flat surface in order to get to solid ground. The only grips are two strong tree roots that have grown within and alongside the surface of the cliff. This Tarzan challenge looks dicey, as I watch the others hold tight the dangling root grips and swing their way onto the other side.

The height of this cliff, and the drop below into even deeper water and sharp rock, do not bode well for me. I tell Philip I am worried, especially in these boots, which offer less than ideal footing and grip. Mostly, though, it is the vast drop, the looming distance below. "Don't look down," Philip tells me, yet again.

"Here, no one looks down. If you don't, you'll be okay." He is sincere and concerned, and knows this spot is a challenging one. From where I stand on the narrow ledge abutting the cliff, I estimate the fall is some 30 to 40 feet. There really is no turning back and, from what I've been told, the most breathtakingly beautiful scenery is yet to come. So, I take a deep breath and firmly grip the cool, smooth vine. It feels thick and sturdy in my hands and gives me some sense of security. Slowly, I make my way along the cliff wall. Grasping for dear life, holding onto the arm-width roots, and using every ounce of strength in my arms, I am able to hoist myself up, swinging, feet bouncing off the cliff face, then down the slippery precipice to safe ground. I cannot believe I have just swung over a 40-foot drop, hanging onto a vine that is growing from the innards of a cliff!

Finally, and with much relief and exhilaration, we reach the jewel of the Mukutan Gorge: the "big waterfall." On this mountaintop, high above the Great Rift Valley, surrounded by the convergence of lush, teal canyons and silver cliffs, the immense waterway spills with a powerful energy and life force into the raging river below. This glorious waterfall, high above the world, rushes a torrent of water into the lower canyon—100 or perhaps 200 feet below us, where a family of baboons hunkers, enjoying the cool, refreshing spray. We have been hiking for a few hours now, and this spot is the perfect place to rest and marvel at nature's pristine beauty. Although everyone else has been here before, especially the guides and rangers of Ol ari Nyiro, they still look around as if witnessing this splendid paradise for the first time. It's a wonderful thing to see: not only the perfection of nature but a unique spot on earth, which inspires such profound awe and wonder.

An Adventure in the Mukutan Gorge

We rest for a while but are mindful of the daylight and the ground that must still be covered. It's not until I stand up that I am aware of my exhaustion. My legs are incredibly weak, the boots feeling like tonnage. Conserving our limited water, I have had only a few sips from the small canteens over the course of the hours we have hiked. I'm worried. While we rested, I removed my boots and found my feet bleeding. Many blisters had formed and popped, and the roominess of the boots created an atmosphere for my feet to scratch, cut, and bleed with every uneasy step onto cliff or across rocks. Pulling the unnatural weight around my ankles too has made my legs weaker than they should be. Knowing that many hours of hiking lay ahead, I can only hope for the best. After a few hours of extreme exertion beneath a raging sun and with little water, I am not feeling as strong as I need to be.

Heading back is nearly unbearable. I say little, reserving my energy, as are the others, taking it slowly as the midday sun continues to weigh heavily upon us. We have managed to retrace our steps and are now hiking through a vast area of thick, tall grass—a spot that is known to harbor many species from big cats to elephant and buffalo. It is imperative that we remain silent in this place where, only days ago, an employee was killed by an elephant.

Just as I am seeing the proverbial light at the end of the tunnel, the head guide veers from the grass plain and into low, thick vegetation, heading into the incline of a mountainside. I have forgotten that the guides promised to take us to see the drawings—the prehistoric cave drawings straight up the side of a mountain. The cave, now, is home to nesting birds of prey. But, evidently, while they hunt and scavenge, the cave remains safe for the viewing.

All this is beside the point. I know my limitations and, by now, I have surpassed them. I am badly dehydrated and exhausted, my heart is pounding rapidly, and it is difficult to catch my breath. But, this moment, in this spot, there is nothing to do but go on. We are in the middle of nowhere, literally, and moving forward is the only way out. The problem is that we are moving sideways, up the steep mountain slope. The vegetation is dense but low, offering no sturdy tree trunks or limbs to hold onto while traversing the mountainside. One by one, we slowly make our way up, stepping through and over thick, damp, jungle foliage. I am panting now and feeling as if my heart is about to explode. I realize that heat stroke is not something to take lightly, and I am fully aware that I am pushing my luck. Many times, each one of us loses footing on the mountainside and slips down—gripping onto anything—branch or bush that will break our fall down the steep decline. We are just feet away from the crest of the mountain where the darkened cave lies, but I cannot make it. The others have somehow lifted their worn bodies up the precipice, scrambling over the ledge and into the cave opening. They coax me along, saying that I can make it—it is only a few more feet—but I cannot move another inch. I have never been so physically challenged in my life, and, while in good shape, I have now pushed the limits of exercise and exertion in the relentless African sun, with very little water for hours.

A few feet from the top, I clench anything that will hold me and keep me anchored enough so as not to fall or slide down the mountain. I am holding on with my last bit of strength, damp earth and vegetation seeming to move all about me. "Please be careful of safari ants," I hear someone say, as I grasp the soil, roots, anything offering solidity. But safari ants, snakes, scorpions, and spiders suddenly become of little or no consequence. For the first time in my life, I have reached a point where I truly do not care what happens next. I think about John, about dying. I think about my own mortality and how fortunate I am to have come back to Africa, alone, to heal. If this was to be the place where I should go—from heat stroke, tumbling down a mountainside, snake bite, whatever— it was simply meant to be. It is an amazing moment, letting go. I sit, my scratched hands and arms grasping anything and everything; feet and legs, caked with dirt and mud, planted firmly into the slope, bracing my weight. I hear everyone talking from inside the darkened cave, echoing voices across ancient stone, amazement at the prehistoric drawings painstakingly carved into cave walls.

My breathing has slowed; my heartbeat calmed. I am warm and tired. I watch insects move in and out of the soil around me. Through the watery sunlight, I see the magnificent birds of prey circling overhead in a sky so bright it hurts my eyes. I smell the life force of the earth, hear the breath of the leaves. I gaze at the majestic mountain opposite me and across the canyon below, at the ethereal scenery that has breathed me into its lungs and swallowed me whole, and cannot believe how beautiful it all is. In resignation, hanging onto a mountain, I am part of a single moment in time. I am part of it all—past, present, and future, all one.

CHAPTER 34

Jeffrey loves the lions Douglas the kudu and gerenuk Philip adores his butterflies ...

It's as large as life and twice as natural.

~ Lewis Carroll

Jeffrey loves the lions. He has great respect for them. He never tires of watching them hunt, feed, and take care of their families. He likes their power, the strength of the family bond. Jeffrey reminds me of a cat. He is very tall, thin, and wiry. You can tell he is strong and capable, quick on his feet. He is proud and self-assured, without being cocky. He knows what he is good at, what he can do. There is strength in the knowing; it garners respect. He is a natural leader and takes good care of those in his watch. When he smiles, he reminds me of the Cheshire Cat. The smile is genuine but gives you the feeling of something more, something you are missing, something up his sleeve. His smile makes me smile. He is quick to laugh, even at himself. That is part of the nobility of the lion. They are comfortable with themselves, in their own skin.

Douglas's favorite animals are the kudu and the gerenuk. I believe I know why he loves the gerenuk so. When they feed — standing on long, hind legs; lifting skyward, tall and graceful, toward the upper limbs and branches — they look like Douglas: soft brown and slim, strong, agile and elegant. Perhaps, in this beautiful animal, he sees his image, and that is good.

There is a lightness of spirit in Philip. Maybe it stems from his devotion to butterflies. All things with wings. He is passionate about beetles and moths, lacewings and dragonflies — all small and light, gauze-like and transparent. They flit and flutter, oftentimes in colors that defy the imagination. They sparkle in sunshine. Some glow at night. They lift into the air when caught in a gentle breeze. I do believe that if Jeffrey, Douglas, and Philip took off in a running flash, it would be Philip who would become airborne and take flight. You can see it in his eyes. When he talks about butterflies, his feet hardly touch the ground.

CHAPTER 35

Reflections

The experience of this sweet life.

~ Dante

The small garden at the camp is profuse with birds. Some of the species include iridescent grackles, sunbirds, black-headed orioles, hoopoes, the go-away bird, whydahs, doves, plovers, Egyptian geese, crested cranes, and parrots. They like to preen and rest in the shade of acacias, fever trees, euphorbia, and eucalyptus.

Are the birds happier at Ol ari Nyiro than other places? Here, birds are singing in flight, each flap of the wing accompanied by a note. It's as if they can't wait to alight on the nearest branch to begin their songs, so they give a preview of sorts in midair ...

Two families of elephants have been raiding the kitchen's organic vegetable garden. The other evening, following dinner, we ran out and into a soft rain to see one family, just feet away, finishing the lettuces. A two-year-old calf was part of the herd. Later that night, in bed with the swirl of bats around my netting, I heard the *askari* yelling at the top of his lungs, pounding his feet into the ground. I could hear him running around the camp, screaming, ending in front of my cottage around 3:00 a.m. The commotion went on for some time, culminating with what sounded like objects being thrown at my cottage, immediately followed by the angry trumpeting of an elephant. My room literally reverberated at the sound, too close for comfort. Seems the *askari* had to frighten off the two families, a total of 15 elephants within the small camp confines. I learned the following morning that the *askari* is "armed" with a bag of stones. This is how he frightens off a three- to four-ton elephant, times 15. A few were eating outside my windows, and he scared them off by pummeling them with small rocks. That was the early-morning ricocheting I heard on my walls. The idea of stone tossing to frighten off the largest land mammal is amazing to me. Better stones than bullets or spears.

The meals prepared in the camp kitchen are some of the most delicious and wholesome I have ever eaten. It is a testimony to the skill and creativity of the head cook, *Mzee* Christopher, and his assistants, fine cooks in their own rights, Elizabeth and Anastasia. All along, I knew that the food was very delicious, *tamu sana*, but I didn't know the limitations of the kitchen that produced such fine meals. I say "limitations" because I am spoiled by too many gadgets, implements, and high-tech appliances, many of them ridiculous and unnecessary, in preparing the most basic of meals.

Today, I am baking two tea cakes — one for the kitchen staff and one for the guides and other employees. *Mzee* Christopher toils in his small, hot kitchen from dawn until well into the night and, with rarely a break from cooking for staff and any guests or volunteers at the research center. I decide it would be nice to give him and the others a short rest while I prepare the ritual of afternoon tea cakes. I've asked permission, and received it, and they have gone to the main camp to get additional flour, sugar, vanilla, and margarine. I think they must be grinning behind my back as they see me flinch and grimace over the cake-making process. There are no cake pans, just two metal bowls. No measuring cups or spoons. This is well and good when cooking savory dishes. But, with the precision of baking, it is a bit more challenging. Eventually, they leave the kitchen to me, except for Elizabeth, who stays on to help and answer questions. The oven door is hanging quite loose on its hinges. It is more off than on. There is no way to set the temperature gauge. Now that I have guessed at all the measurements and poured the batter into bowls rather than pans, I realize the oven door won't shut. Elizabeth assures me that this is not a problem, *hakuna matata*. The oven door is securely fashioned on both sides with thick rope, which is then fastened to the wall. I have no idea at what temperature the cakes are baking and no idea how long to bake them.

Overall, the cakes turn out just fine and are served at tea. They are a bit salty, as I didn't realize they use only salted margarine whereas I use sweet butter. No one complains, and they are eaten, happily. Naturally, I am not thrilled with the outcome, but I suppose they were good enough because Philip has asked me if it is possible for him to prepare this cake on the single-stove burner in his cottage. I tell him that I don't think he can make this like a griddle cake, so he asks for the next best thing: Will I make another cake for him tomorrow? Either they like salty cakes or these are the most gracious people I have ever met.

Douglas tells me that, about a month ago, he awoke to a spitting cobra making its way into his room through an open window. He stood on his bed as the snake slowly moved across the floor and was able to jump out the window to get help. My room is not far from his. I picture the open, chicken-wire construction at the top of my walls. Fondly, I think of the clumsy bats and abundance of guano, and, suddenly, their antics don't seem so bad. A spitting cobra? This is the kind of anecdote I prefer to get when I'm packed and the motor is running, not when I have another week to go ...

The winds pick up as the sun melts into the horizon. I can smell rain. Heavy clouds cast shadows across the hills and, from somewhere below, deep in the canyons, I hear baboons barking. It has rained nearly every day since my arrival at Ol ari Nyiro, usually at night when I am beneath my bed covers. Rain is unusual for August, they say; this is the dry season. Perhaps the "short rains" of November and December have arrived early. In any event, they are grateful. Soon enough, the skies will dry out, and the land will become parched and yellow. Rain is valuable, Jeffrey assures me. "We are always thankful for a little rain."

It is cold tonight. Before dinner, I join Jeffrey and the cooks outside the kitchen where they are warming themselves beside a fire of burning coals. The heat rises to a blurred, watery vision, seeping into the many hands hovering above the hot embers. The heat feels good against the damp, and the smells of *Mzee* Christopher's dinner whet our appetites. Tonight, he has prepared freshly caught talapia. He has sautéed it with tomatoes and garlic, a handful of fresh herbs. There are potatoes and fresh green beans, salad. Always, and in the center of the table, are tiny, olive-wood bowls filled with fresh sea salt and pepper and crushed chilies. With the cool rain falling outside, the candlelight, good friends, and a delicious, home-cooked meal, I am lulled into a sense of home, of family.

After dinner, Jeffrey, Douglas, the two volunteers, and I relax in the sitting room. A red-hot fire is blazing in the stone hearth; candles and kerosene lamps provide additional lighting. Elizabeth has lit sticks of incense. The rain is falling in steady streams now. We talk for some hours, mostly hearing tales about the hazards of the local brew, *changaa*, which can be debilitating if not fatal. The brew is notorious for blinding and killing many Kenyans, as it is often spiked with ethanol, and pure fuel. And, at just a few shillings a glass, it is the cheapest way to imbibe or get drunk in no time flat. Drunk, only if you are fortunate. Most of the time, Douglas and Jeffrey tell us, it slams you into a state of oblivion, but only after the vomiting has consumed you. And that's if you are lucky. With a poverty level in Kenya at around 60%, many Kenyans can only afford the local brew. In many cases, you do not know what you are getting when you order *changaa*, whether or not your brew has been tainted or laced with ethanol. Because it is such a cheap drink and widely available, mass consumption is inevitable. During my previous trip to Kenya, I had heard similar stories of many impoverished Kenyans unknowingly receiving the poisonous concoction. Attempts are being made to make *changaa* illegal due to the lethal side effects. So, tonight, as we sip herb chai before the fire, tea has never tasted so good.

On my foot safaris, a few of the animals I have encountered: elephant, buffalo, warthogs, impala, zebra, Coke's hartebeest, waterbuck, hyena, rabbits, bat-eared fox, black mamba, leopard-back tortoise, and puff adder. On my birthday, Jeffrey and I took a short walking safari, about 11 miles, with a young Turkana *askari*, Joseph. We nearly stepped on a young black mamba that slithered across our path. It was a lovely, small snake, quite delicate looking. The bush is thick with snakes from the mamba and puff adder to pythons and cobras. Black mambas injure more people simply due to the snake's prolific numbers; however, the bite of the puff adder is far more deadly. Days later, while hiking down a mountain in the Mukutan Gorge, Douglas nearly stumbles onto a slow-moving puff adder halfway into our descent. They are not fast but rather thick and slow. I watch as it moves its way past, not far from Douglas's feet, and into the dense mountain foliage. Only moments before, I sat, gripping the mountainside so as not to tumble downwards, oblivious to many of the hidden dangers that may have moved alongside me. The reality of wildlife, though, is that, for the most part, it will avoid you at all costs. Animals are at their most dangerous when threatened, startled, or frightened. If it can, the wild will avoid a confrontation long before you are ever aware of its presence. It simply prefers to be left alone.

CHAPTER 36

A Tent on the Edge of the World

Sand-strewn caverns, cool and deep,
Where the winds are all asleep.

~ Matthew Arnold

There are some things in life that cannot be fully described in words. Places so beautiful or spiritually profound, they defy conventional description, and thought process and words only diminish the splendor of what lies ahead. These rare places can only be felt, and the very feeling becomes the experience—the fluttering in the chest, the lump in the throat, the overwhelming sense of peace and belonging—all telling you that you have happened upon a sacred place, where only the heart and spirit can speak so eloquently.

This place, the view that stretches before me and from my tent and verandah, is Makena's Hills. I stand in the warmth of the sun, beneath a soft, blue sky. To my left is Lake Baringo, a shimmering vision of milky white, while in front of me lays the Great Rift Valley of which Baringo is a part. The Rift Valley stretches for hundreds of miles, layers upon layers of undulating hills, volcanic mountain peaks, gorges and plateaus in shades of green and teal and muted purple. Before that, still, is a wave of tall, yellow prairie grasses tilting in the breeze, clumps of wild sage half hidden behind the sea of golden grass, and an occasional tree breaking up an otherwise endless stretch of valley ahead.

Alongside the grass is a narrow pathway that leads to wide, stone steps and up to the hardwood verandah. Carved posts from local trees adorn the front space; trailing vines of fragrant jasmine wind and drape around each post. From the posts hang kerosene lanterns that stay illuminated throughout the night to discourage passersby of the four-legged kind. On the verandah is a small table, also carved from a tree, and two canvas chairs. It is from those seats that I look upon a prehistoric landscape that feeds, nurtures, and rejuvenates the soul, and that previous words could not begin to describe.

The "room" at night (it is in fact a tent, but one would never know this until the winds fire up from both sides of the valley, shaking the canvas walls and ceiling and sending the large, Moroccan lantern swaying from its ribbon) takes on a mystical, ethereal mood when lit by the many brass lamps. Candles and the soft scent of burning incense make the space dreamlike in the flickering shadow and light. From my bed, and behind layers of billowing mosquito netting, I look out and onto the golden light of the lanterns, creating fluid shapes on the soft walls, and listen to the winds fingering their way along the canvas flaps. At this moment, fully awake, the vision of white net clouds and dancing firelight is far more magical than any dream.

I would be remiss if I didn't mention perhaps the most spectacular feature of my canvas room. Attached to the main tent is a luxurious bathroom with hardwood floor, double sinks, and a massive stone tub from which I can look at the African landscape. The huge window, which runs the length of the tub, is permanently open to the wild; no glass, no nothing between you and the swaying yellow grass and the soft highland breeze. On the counter is a glass decanter filled with the rich, emerald oil of wild leleshwa. Solar-heated water is available, but limited and precious, so a steamy bath filled with the rich sage oil is a luxury and a treat. To slip into a natural-stone bath of deep-green color and herbal fragrance, while the scents of the plains, the valleys, the mountains, and the animals waft through and against your bare skin, is a singularly sensuous experience. The only sounds come from birds and insects, the wind rustling through the grasses, or a distant snort of some unknown animal. My senses in this warm, fragrant bath are heightened, and, for many reasons, not the least being naked and submerged with the wild at your fingertips and the instinctual feeling of vulnerability should something with fur or claws, scales or wings decide to join you. That said, there's nothing lovelier than a soak while gazing upon a vast, primordial landscape, and I would gladly slip into that stone tub at any time and greet a hoofed passerby with a relaxed hello. (A bull buffalo might be the exception.)

The majority of my time here is spent on the verandah or in my tent, my own private world. Everything around me is a feast for the senses: the softness underfoot of the jewel-toned kilims scattered about my tent; the incessant trill and buzz of insects; the sweet perfume of jasmine blossoms mixed with the earthy scent of the prairie grasses and soil. And then there is the view. It's the first time in many years that I have felt such a sense of calm and tranquility. There is a peacefulness about this land, this spot. It offers a clarity of mind and spirit that seems to fill the lungs with every breath taken from the warm valley breeze. You can feel the very pulse of the land. It is alive.

After a light breakfast, a solitary stroll around the camp, and writing, Ali brings a delicious lunch to my tree table: samosas, roast chicken, mesclun salad and sliced tomatoes, papaya, and good white wine. Full and satiated, it's time for a brief but healing nap, cut short by the rhythmic tapping of raindrops on my canvas ceiling. Soon, Douglas will arrive at my tent for an early-evening bush drive. The light rain continues to fall, more a thin veil of drizzle, which does not hamper our time in this wilderness paradise. In the silvery mist and on open land, many elephants have collected to browse, one last chance at full bellies before the rain becomes heavy and they must retreat into thicker bush for cover. Just a few meters down the road, and not far from a small herd of elephants, rests a pride of seven lions. They are lying in a single line, side by side, two adult females and five subadults. They lull, lazily, but, soon enough and as darkness swallows the twilight, they will ready themselves for the hunt. We leave them to their last few moments of repose before the energy of the hunt begins, and set off for a higher vantage point to take in the last of the waning daylight. From our mountaintop rest, we look upon volcanic Lake Baringo as the final shafts of filtered sunlight illuminate the alkaline lake before night falls. Here, above the Rift, storm clouds approach, moving quickly. Just as the dying sun casts its final glow across the landscape, dusk gives way, the moon alights, and we head back to camp.

As all trips do, this one has taken on a life of its own and one unexpected. I had come back to Kenya to heal. To be at one with my beloved African wilderness, the bush, the animals, the peace and spirituality of this unique spot on the planet. One year after John's death, I found that my solo trip of new beginnings and healing spirit was also one of newfound friendships. And, through my new Kenyan friends, I have learned much and made heartfelt connections. How fortunate I've been. Whether trekking deep within the bush, or sharing evening conversation around firelight, they have given me a rare glimpse into the real Kenya, not just the Kenya perceived by tourists. These people are some of the most insightful and gracious individuals I have ever known. They are kind and generous, shockingly honest and straightforward. They have told me about their families and ethnic groups. Whether Kikuyu, Luo, Turkana, or Meru, they are all proud and good people. There is a depth of wisdom in many of my new friends — a wisdom far beyond their years. In some respects, they grow up faster here. Life is not easy. They seem to have a deeper understanding of the world and their place within it than do so many young adults from Western cultures. Somehow, I sense, they have found a balance between planning for their futures, the futures of their families, and living for the present, the moment. Life is precious. I have been privileged, this trip. I found an extended family of sorts halfway around the world. And the genuine kinship we have shared, coming on the heels of losing my family, John, moves and humbles me.

The evening has me feeling bittersweet, my last night at Ol ari Nyiro. I have been here now for a few weeks, between the research center and Makena's Hills, all part of this sprawling, 100,000-acre wildlife reserve in the remote Laikipia wilderness. My time here has been healing in myriad ways, and more than I could have imagined or hoped for. I have been looked after, taken care of. Taking care of — one of the greatest gifts a human being can give to another. It has been a long time. *Asante Sana*.

So tonight, relaxed and tired, I take dinner at my tent, the usual spot on the carved-tree table; brass lanterns and candles glowing around me; the dark, crisp night air filled with indistinguishable noises and animal scents riding on the breeze. I need this time, the final days of my Kenyan trip, to let everything sink in, to reflect. With the wind beginning to howl, dinner finished, I absorb this solitary moment, deep in the African bush, alone but for the moon and stars and nocturnal creatures.

I sit at the small writing desk in my tent, the winds blowing through the canvas flaps. The desk is illuminated by lantern, night table with candles, the flames jumping and flickering with each blast of wind. By this soft-yellow light, I write and read about buffalo and lions, elephants and rhino, all part of this timeless beauty around me. This moment could be one from any time, long ago. Changeless scenery, unaffected by the hands of man, a view and landscape little changed in a thousand years. I could be anyone, from long ago, sitting too by candlelight or kerosene lamp at a small writing desk, chronicling the day's adventures in the bush—the same scorching African sun, the same biting winds of the Rift at night, the very same moon and stars, the shared excitement of being in the heart of the wild—from where it all began. I have been here before. I will be here again.

I am grateful.

CHAPTER 37

An Oasis on Lake Naivasha

Paradise is where I am.

~ Voltaire

Depending on weather, potholes, herds of cattle and goats, or obstinate baboons relaxing in the middle of the road, it is a dusty four- to five-hour drive southward from the Laikipia region and Ol ari Nyiro to the green, fertile banks of Lake Naivasha. Just a bit over an hour outside of Nairobi, Lake Naivasha is a tropical paradise, lush with fever trees and papyrus, bursts of blinding color from bougainvillea, candle bush, and hibiscus. The air sits heavy with the sweet perfume of jasmine and China roses.

The staff at Olerai House has been anticipating my arrival. I'm very late, and they are happy to see me. I am the only guest after all, and they have prepared a late-afternoon lunch. Monica leads me across the garden to my cottage. The king-size bed is strewn with hot-pink bougainvillea blossoms. A comfortable banquette built into the huge bay window overlooks the expanse of gardens, fever trees, and a small lagoon that attracts not only the resident zebra herd but monkeys, fish eagles and Egyptian geese.

Outside, lunch is served on a long, linen-draped table facing the gardens and grassland. Above, in the dense, fever-tree canopy, vervet monkeys sit patiently, watching for what might be up for grabs, as do the iridescent starlings. Deborah and Miriam bring lunch, lovingly prepared by the chef, Njoki (or Big Mama, as they call her). After the long drive, I am hungry. The food is nothing short of sublime. Generous helpings of antipasti are fanned across bright, ceramic platters; prosciutto and melon; assorted cheeses; juicy, ripe tomatoes; homemade breads; a glass of fresh passion juice. I am pleasantly full but, to my surprise, the parade of dishes continues with a savory, hot artichoke gratin, green bean and herb salad, warm herbed zucchini, and a mixed lettuce salad—all fresh, organic produce grown on the grounds. The food is delicious, and I can't help but feel uncomfortable that such time and effort have gone into preparing so many dishes for only one guest—and more than I can possibly eat. I'm reassured by Miriam that the abundance of food is due to last-minute cancellations. Hopefully, the leftovers will happily be eaten by the staff. Here, I am sure, nothing goes to waste.

It is often a difficult pill to swallow during travel when trying to juggle the reality of abundance and overindulgence, with a population for whom finding enough food to survive is an ongoing struggle. With a poverty rate of over 60%, Kenya is a country with vast and varied problems, perhaps the most important being hunger, malnutrition, and disease borne from thus. While tourism sustains the economy and provides the livelihoods for many Kenyans who would otherwise be unemployed, it is tough for both the heart and head to find a comfortable place—a balance of extremes. Maybe the whole point is not to find a comfortable place, in the status quo, as it does not and should not exist. I do know that most of the places I have stayed within the country use much of the tourist dollar not only for employee salaries but toward education and healthcare in the local communities, as well as conservation issues. Naturally, this is not true with all destinations, but it makes the bitter pill a bit easier to get down. Guilt will get us nowhere, but, hopefully, realization, acknowledgement, and action will move us toward a solution.

The zebra herd has moved closer and seems to enjoy grazing near my table. The brazen starlings, on the other hand, are not as well mannered and land smack dab in the middle of the plates. They are quick to grab a corner of bread, a leftover ball of melon, anything they can get their beaks around before I can shoo them away. They are beautiful birds and, up close in full sunlight, their feathers are shimmering in tints of watery pink and lavender, turquoise and soft blue.

After lunch, I take a long walk around the gardens. The main house—a small, enchanting cottage—is draped with climbing vines and flowers, so thick one wonders if the house didn't sprout from the fecund soil. Standing guard around the cottage, a trail of wispy, yellow acacias, a smattering of fever trees, and an ancient fig complement the sun-dappled surrounds. The natural placement of trees offers pools of shade without enveloping the entire garden and grassland in shadow. Where brilliant sunlight fingers its way between limbs and leaves, hedges burst with tropical flowers; large, earthenware pots and other assorted vessels overflow with fragrant lavender and leggy geraniums. The massive fig tree, which looms next to my room, is perhaps 75 feet high and appears nearly as wide—a formidable girth, more like a wall of bark than a trunk. The vervet family enjoys playing in this jungle of a tree, scrambling up and down its base and limbs, hiding in the canopy, awaiting the ripening of the fruit. The baboons too will arrive soon enough, when the figs ripen to taste, as the bounty of the tree will provide enough fruit for everyone.

The day slips quickly by, and evening rapidly envelopes after a short fanfare of dusk. Straddling the equator does not allow for lingering twilight. Vibrant colors explode and quickly disappear, fading into hazy tones of what once was. Just as one's eyes adjust to the impossible shades of scarlet and coral and burning pink, darkness swallows the sky whole, and color is replaced by the light of a million stars.

Simeon, the manager, has lit a fire in the cozy sitting room of the main cottage. It is cool tonight, as it has been most nights on this trip. Winter, even in Africa, can get quite cold. While it's balmier along the lake region than it was in the highlands of Laikipia, there is still a bite to the evening air. It is time for dinner and, although lunch could have sustained me for the entire day, or two, Njoki has prepared yet another incredible meal. Deborah has set a small table for one in front of the fire. I have a few minutes before dinner is ready, so I sit on a low, carved wooden stool in front of the flames.

Again, I am the only guest. The U.S. State Department warnings seem to have accomplished their goal of needlessly frightening away tourists, and Olerai House too had a rush of last-minute cancellations. In a country that is dependent on tourist dollars for its very survival, Kenya has suffered greatly. Many Kenyans believe that the U.S. warnings were more a punishment of sorts, as the Kenyan government objected to, and refused to enforce, many of President George W. Bush's "demands" regarding antiterrorism tactics and mandates following 9/11.

The owners of Olerai, whom I had hoped to meet, are up north in the Samburu reserve. They are the renowned elephant experts, Oria and Iain Douglas-Hamilton, of Save the Elephants.

When I was young, I was introduced to their documentaries on African elephants and watched how they raised their two daughters alongside the herds. They have written numerous books about elephant behavior, were instrumental in the banning of the ivory trade, and are respected worldwide for their tireless conservation efforts. So, I am alone at their guest cottage on the lake while they are in Samburu where they operate Elephant Watch Safaris and a small, tented retreat, Elephant Camp, which I understand sits empty as well. At least they can continue their elephant monitoring and research, although absent tourist dollars will not help pay for staff or replenish the account for ongoing conservation and study.

Deborah brings in a bottle of red wine and tells me that dinner is ready. Undoubtedly, Njoki is one of the finest chefs I have come across. As someone who loves food and loves to cook, I would have to say that her cooking is nothing short of perfection and perhaps the best I have had the privilege to eat. Tonight, she has prepared a creamy vegetable soup, freshly caught talapia with green-olive tapenade, herbed rice, and a sauté of baby vegetables, which include haricots verts, snap peas, carrots, and corn, with a handful of fresh herbs. For dessert, stewed green mango with lightly sweetened cream. She is a wizard, this woman. Not only must you possess great skill, but you must also love what you are doing to create such food. The bounty of what is taken from the soil and the waters seems to blossom into something greater than it once was, when lovingly and creatively combined with one other, and at the magic touch of Njoki's hands.

After dinner, I visit the kitchen for conversation with the four women on staff. Monica, Miriam, Deborah, and Njoki are indeed spoiling me with their easygoing nature and humor. I can't help but think they feel a little relieved not to have a full house. But they do not have to go out of their way in offering such heartfelt kindness and effort, and I've told them so. I am here, alone, to unwind and "just be"; to enjoy the beauty of the country and its people. I really don't need or want to be indulged, although I am grateful for their attention and care. For many reasons on this trip, I simply wanted to blend with the landscape, breathe the same air as the elephant and the fish eagle, feel the same soil beneath my feet as the lion and the umbrella thorn. The additional gifts I have received — kindness and honesty, friendship and humor — have gone far beyond any expectation, unexpected in its selfless generosity.

Just as I'm contemplating if Njoki's kitchen isn't in fact paradise, Simeon rushes into the room with a flashlight and says I must come with him to see a hippo that has just lumbered into the garden. Only a few feet away and beneath a full, wavering moon, a large, male hippo casually grazes on a flowering hedge just a stone's throw from the kitchen door. It is a long way from the lake and canal, but, still, the hippos make a nightly pilgrimage to the house and gardens for delicacies not available along the banks. Or is it the intoxicating scents that waft from Njoki's kitchen? Simeon tells me that the same walking path used by the owners and guests from the house to the canal is used by the hippo too. Obviously, the hippos see the convenience of the path as an open invitation to graze the delectable vegetation growing outside the house and cottages.

The hippo is a remarkable creature, a mass of naked, gray bulk, short-legged and squat, and yet amazingly agile and powerful. Their canines are deadly, and it is not uncommon for a small boat or canoe to be bitten in half with very little effort

275

should it get in the way or prove threatening. Hippos are responsible for more human deaths in Africa than any other animal, except for the mosquito and snake. You do not want to find yourself between a landlocked hippo and water, nor do you want to flaunt yourself in an aggressive bull's territory, especially in a small vessel. While classified as herbivores or grazers, on rare occasion, and witnessed by researchers during a wildebeest migration along the Mara River, hippos have been known to eat flesh, floating carrion left behind or moving downriver after being taken by crocodiles or trampled during the mass river crossings.

At bedtime, the elderly *askari* walks me across the expansive gardens toward my room, armed with a flashlight. "Hippo," he says, "come very close to your room." He shakes the flashlight for effect. Somehow, this elderly gentleman, armed with a small flashlight, doesn't appear very intimidating to me. I can't imagine he'd frighten off a pack of dwarf mongoose, let alone an irritated hippo. Nevertheless, he knows better than I. More than likely, he has lived his many years in the company of these massive creatures, both in the lake and along its shores. But, in knowing the strength and agility of the hippo, and as I have felt when in close proximity to the elephant, I am greatly humbled and respectful of their power and sense of place. I suppose, though, if an *askari* can frighten away a family of elephants from outside my room at Ol ari Nyiro with a handful of small stones, then perhaps it is just what it takes to frighten off an aggressive, few-thousand-pound hippo—a good smack to the head with a tiny torch. How I wish all conflicts between man and animal could be dealt with such mutual respect and benign fashion.

Next morning, Simeon and I walk the hippo path down to the canal and the awaiting gondola. Tended by two young Masai, the bright-turquoise gondola is adorned with layers of papyrus and pink, yellow and orange bougainvillea, appearing as if it blossomed and was cut loose from the fertile banks. With the Masai at the bow and stern, and Simeon and I in the middle, we steer down the narrow canal toward the mouth of Lake Naivasha. Slowly, navigating through the jungle-like channel, a canopy of thick papyrus drapes over each sliver of shore, casting dark shadows on the spongy banks. The vegetation is lush and moist; a tangle of candle-bush blossoms, in a profusion of burning yellow, flank the calm, emerald waters. Flowers and buds the colors of confetti burst from the depths of the glistening fronds, while kingfishers flit and hover over the reflective surface of the water, darting at prospective meals. Alighting in various tiers of the canopy are plovers, massive fish eagles, and ibis.

Leaving behind the soft-green ribbon of water, we glide, effortlessly, across the vast, open surface of an opalescent Naivasha. In the distance, through a milky haze, is the blurred, purple outline of Mount Longonot — the towering, benevolent presence of an extinct volcano, holding court along the shores of the lake. To my immediate left, and seemingly not so benign, is a pod of 15 hippos, lumped together in an unbroken chain of monstrous, pinkish-gray bulk. A sea of tiny ears, twitching above the waterline and planted atop massive heads, look dwarfed and out of proportion against the profusion of gigantic muzzles and necks. They are noisy animals, hippos, and, as we move nearer, their low-density grunts and honks vibrate across and beneath the water's surface. Admittedly, the hippopotamus makes me nervous. Granted, I have watched far too many documentaries on the "dark side" of hippo behavior. For the most part, these incredible and oddly beautiful animals are nonthreatening, but you don't want to intimidate or taunt, especially if calves are present or territorial bulls. From where I sit, the gondola suddenly seems toy-like, a Lilliputian vessel in a sea of snorting giants. I am secretly praying that I only witness the light side of the hippo — the family-oriented, good-natured demeanor of this huge, amphibious mammal. After a mock charge by a bull, I am greatly relieved when we steer away from the family and into deeper waters.

The iridescent lake is teeming with pelicans and cormorants perched on mooring posts, while smaller water birds and fowl skim and bob along the surface, creating tiny wakes across the glistening face. An opportunistic fish eagle flies overhead, looking for an easy meal. In the still, cool, morning air, the long view, now toward a faraway shore, is soft and dream-like, muted by a line of mist and fog lifting off the warm lake waters. Behind the billowy haze rise multitiered layers of hills and mountains, both jagged and softly undulating, a tapestry of whitewashed color in quieted tones of purple, blue, and sage green.

Small, I sit in the middle of an ancient lake, surrounded by a timeless landscape. I cannot stop thinking of John. How he would have loved this place, Kenya. Gliding across an endless stretch of shimmering lake; silent, save for the hushed sounds of aquatic life; empty, but for a smattering of distant fishing boats. And, the tiny brushstroke of a brilliant, turquoise gondola covered with bright-pink flowers, where rifts of flute and song flit across primordial waters, as baby hippos frolic on the backs of their submerged mothers, seemingly dancing on the water's surface.

South Africa ~ 2004

Time passed. Eventually I wandered back along the forest trail and scrambled down behind my house to the beach. The sun was a huge red orb just vanishing behind the Congo hills and I sat on the beach watching the ever-changing sunset as it painted the sky red and gold and dark purple. The surface of the lake, calm after the storm, glinted gold and violet and red ripples below the flaming sky.

~ Jane Goodall, *Reason for Hope*

CHAPTER 38

In the Darkness, Red and Black

The soul of a man is larger than the sky,
Deeper than the ocean, or the abysmal dark
Of the unfathomed center.

~ David Hartley Coleridge

I don't remember if we were heading back from Cape Town or Stellenbosch. And I suppose it doesn't matter. It was night, rather late, and we were tired. We were on the mountain pass heading toward Franschhoek and a tiny, rental cottage.

The pass, by day, is like a beautiful dream. It is high drama in deep violet and earthy sage. It is carved into towering mountainsides terraced with grapevines, and, when not hidden by waves of fog and cloud, the jagged peaks are dusted in purple shadows. By nightfall, however, all is unseen. Color disappears. No lights other than a passing headlight; only darkness, concealing the hunkering stone and ledge that flanks the roadway. There are four lanes, two in each direction. I didn't like this road at night for one reason only: the darkness. It was as if you were hurtling into space; nothing before or behind you, just eerily still darkness and whatever chanced to move about in its grasp. My fear too was that some wild animal would run into the roadway—a dog, a rabbit, perhaps a baboon. I never thought anything else would fall prey to the darkness of the mountain pass.

From behind, we heard sirens. We slowed down and pulled into the left lane. In South Africa, one drives on the opposite side of the road. The blaring sirens came closer and passed us, vanishing into blackness. Just a few kilometers up the pass, we saw motionless vehicles. Two emergency vehicles were parked in the center of the lanes, one civilian car to the far right, along the side of the road. Bright-orange cones were peppered between lanes. It was dark, but I could see enough from the lights of the vehicles ahead. "Don't look!" he said. But it was too late.

I remember the stillness. Everything was eerily still. I saw no movement anywhere. Then I saw a man walk back toward the ambulance. But what struck me was how very quiet it all was — no sound, no screaming, no shrieks of pain, of panic. Nothing. Other than my own breath, sound ceased to exist.

To my right was a body. In the shadowy darkness, it lay in the center of the road. He was tall and thin. He had long, black legs; I remember them. They were very thin. He was barefoot. No one stood nearby. There was no one with him. He was surrounded with orange cones. A thin, black body circled by bright-orange cones. I mostly remember the thinness of his legs. Then, in slow motion, my eyes moved upward and, in that fleeting moment when our car slowly pulled away, I saw red. I don't know what it was. I thought it was a piece of red fabric covering his face, but I am not sure. It could have been blood. It could have been where his head should have rested, and now only blood. But it was red. Even in the deep mountains of darkness and fog, I saw red.

Later, I realized he must have been dead. That could be the only explanation as to why no one was near him, aiding him, comforting him. And why all was quiet. He was gone. He had left home that day in shorts and bare feet. He was probably heading home after a long day of work. He had no other option but to cross those ominous lanes in utter darkness, a chance he surely took many times before. Heading home. Dinner was waiting. Maybe, I like to believe, a warm fire would have welcomed him. Family.

They are poor in these villages. There are people who only walk. They walk to work and to school, and everywhere in between. They walk in the scorching heat of the sun, biting wind, pelting rain, the black of night. And, ultimately, they must contend with the darkness. They must battle nightfall, fog, and shadow. They blend with the night. This night, he became one with the darkness of the mountain pass. Only after he joined the mountain's shadow did color appear out of the void. Orange and red.

I prefer those colors in wildflowers.

I never heard or read anything about the man who was hit. Did he have a wallet, identification on him? How long before his family, home with dinner waiting, heard a knock on the door? How long before the mountain darkness enveloped their home that had been bright and warm, burning red with firelight?

The darkness of that mountain pass became even darker that night.

CHAPTER 39

Hope in a Sea of Gray

Enough is as good as a feast.

~ Heywood

Cape Town, even in winter, is an exuberance of color and energy. It has more than its share of natural riches in the beauty of sea and sand and mountains. It bursts with fragrant flowers and flowering trees. An artist's delight in washes of azure, turquoise and teal, purples and greens, and the chalky white of beach and cloud. And bright-sunshine yellow. Embellished with broad strokes of red, orange, and ochre; quieted with touches of pink and lavender, heathered mauve. All in the forms of wildflowers and fynbos. Scrub and oak. Miles of towering mountains and white-sand beaches.

Outside of Cape Town and just a few kilometers away lay the rich, fertile Winelands. The richness of the region is apparent in the vast stretches of vineyards, fruit orchards, and olive groves. There is a depth of color to this land. Shades become heavier, richer, perhaps due to the weight of so much fruit. There is a concentration to the color of the Winelands, a tonal difference that may be attributed to land shaded by mountains as opposed to the sun's reflection off the sea.

It is what lies between where color fades. Where the lavish landscapes of dense color begin to mute, eventually bleeding to gray. They say that gray is a color. Here, I would beg to disagree. Here, I would say it's more of a feeling. A sense. A cloudiness of conscience until the color of reality sets in. Only then does the gray become color and blindingly clear. This is a line of earth that is sketched and scribbled in lead-pencil gray. The box of color, for the most part, was not availed here. What I saw was a wash of gray mostly borne from discarded scrap metal.

It is a strong dose of reality when one sees the townships for the first time — witnesses the townships — the shanties or slums abutting Cape Town. In either direction, you leave behind worlds of abundance and privilege only to see a very different reality, what lives in between those pockets. Built on soft ground, unstable dunes, and often flooded in downpours, the shanty towns or squatters' camps (whatever one chooses to call them) stretch for miles along the highway that connects the beautiful city on the sea to the valleys of wine. Thousands upon thousands of men, women, and children live in "houses" that are nothing more than discarded materials: corrugated steel, twisted sheet metal, cardboard boxes, and plastic garbage bags, all of which act as makeshift barriers against the rain and cold. The areas I saw were mainly without electricity and water. Some of the townships have limited power and shared toilet facilities, but the shanties and camps I regularly passed had no basic services. Mile after mile was nothing more than ramshackle construction, what looked like the forts and tents that children erect at play, with nothing more than found objects lying around yards and streets. But this is not play. Within these cardboard walls are families. Beneath the roofs of rusted sheet metal are human beings. Surely, there is color inside, unseen. But, from the outside, and in every sense of the meaning, these camps are a sobering dose of human suffering, and the profound dichotomy of the haves and have-nots.

I have flown over the slums of Nairobi and seen impoverished shanty towns deep in the Kenyan countryside. But, witnessing the shanties on the fringes of Cape Town, on many occasions and closer yet, I felt a sense of hopelessness. Why can't we, the collective we, find answers and solutions for so many? I know it's complex. I know there are more dimensions and facets of poverty than I can possibly comprehend. But how can we allow so many to live cold and hungry, endangered by disease, the elements, and other desperate human beings? The gray is palpable.

Each time I drove past, I felt a wave of emotion: shame, guilt, sorrow, profound sadness, empathy, compassion, frustration, ignorance, and deep gratitude for all I have. It is one of those things that makes no sense in this world and has not since the beginning of time. How, I wondered, did so many desperate people find the strength to go on? What made thousands, millions of people, living in varying degrees of poverty, get up each day and face a world that appeared to offer so little hope? It made me wonder about the human spirit, the levels of "living," what I thought of as survival, the will to live, and hope.

I thought of my own profound losses—the losses of my father, close friends, my husband, other family members, all while I was relatively young—and I wondered what it was that gave us the motivation to go on. There are many days when I struggle to find meaning, to find reason to hope. But, in witnessing the townships and camps, I realized that my personal losses, no matter how profound, were nothing compared to the stretch of concentrated suffering before me. I have never known how it feels to be hungry and cold in addition to losing those I love. If nothing more, and selfishly, this area of gray made certain things in life all the clearer.

I saw the highway flanked with children, playing along the narrow strips of sandy soil and scrub grasses. They were playing soccer, dragging sticks, hanging out with friends. As the cars sped by, these children and young adults of the shanties seemed to relish the fresh air, the feel of the soil beneath their bare feet. Many were laughing. Other inhabitants of the camps were heading home after a long day of labor. Exhaustion was imprinted on their faces, but one last effort had to be made in crossing the four lanes of traffic, heading home. Heading home to cardboard and metal. On the older faces, I saw fewer smiles.

As I drove by the last stretch of this shanty town, something jumped out from the colorless line. At the very end of the camp was one particularly run-down shack. It is hard to imagine that one shack — all constructed of ripped cardboard, rusted metal, and torn plastic — could look even worse than the next. But this last house did, until I realized what had caught my eye. This house of many angles but none being at 90 degrees, lopsided, falling apart, and seemingly ready to collapse, had a solid, wood door. And not just any door. This shack, built between a few gnarled trees and abutting the highway, had a painted door. Somehow, the owner of this shack had gotten hold of leftover paint. Red paint. It was carried home and painted, rather neatly too, across the face of the withered, wood door. What happened that day, the day of the painted door, was extraordinary.

Survival is often nothing more than instinct. During the worst of times, it is what gets us up, moving, fed and watered, and back to sleep. It is instinctual to all living things. Some are better at it than others. And some don't make it, no matter how hard they try. The will to live, in my eyes, is something different. It is experienced by beings of intellect and reason. It is a kick-start that says, "I must go on. I will go on," no matter how horrific the circumstance might be. It is more than mere survival, of finding food and shelter and warmth. It is a conscious effort—the will of mind, body, and spirit—that says, "I will live," regardless of what it takes. However, if on a particularly promising day, if one finds a discarded bucket of bright-red paint, then the color of hope emerges. Like a mysterious flower, hope blooms out of the direst of circumstances. Hope is what is borne after a night of cold and hunger, a night of loneliness and pain, when you wish for nothing more than permanent sleep. It is the morning after the longest night when you wake up with an unexpected lightness of being. It is that day when you tell your children they will have more than this; their lives will be better. And, most important, you will see to it. It is the morning when you look at a lopsided front door, find a bucket of red paint, and say, "I think I might like a bright-red door. A bright-red door would look beautiful."

Hope is the cherry on the sundae. Even when there is no sundae. It is the tiny, sweet thing we save for last. When we've gotten through the surviving, the will to live, and finally made our way to the sweet taste of the cherry.

This day, that is what emerged from the sketch of lead-pencil gray. From the lopsided shack at the end of the shanty on the side of the highway. Hope is the bright-red door.

CHAPTER 40

Calla Lilies

Remember that the most beautiful things in the world are the most useless; peacocks and lilies for instance.

~ John Ruskin

As a child, in our tiny rental house, I remember seeing them for the first time. They lined either side of the narrow, gravel driveway, and from my bedroom window they looked like giant, prehistoric flowers, standing guard over the pathway. "They're calla lilies," my mother told me. But the name didn't have the same effect on me as did the unique beauty of this strange moonflower.

I don't recall when I saw other flowers for the first time: lavender, wisteria, lilacs, and roses — all favorites, but no remembrance of my initial encounters. The calla lily, however, stood out. It wasn't like the other blossoms. It was formidable yet delicate; a hearty stalk; a solid, thick skin; a sturdy pistil and one huge bowl of a bloom. There wasn't an abundance of petals and frills, or things that easily dropped off or blew away in a gentle wind. There was never a collection of dainty blossoms around my feet when I touched and investigated this odd flower. Yet, in its solidity, there was delicacy too. The strength of that creamy cup gave way, just at the tip, to a fragile-looking curl, a sweep, a downward taper that seemed to be where the lily shed her tears when the morning dew was particularly heavy. Sometimes, in the morning, I would catch one last tear; one perfect, crystal prism catching the sunlight; a diamond resting at the very edge, the tip, and like magic it would evaporate in the strengthening sun.

There is a fragrance to the calla lily. Most people would disagree, but it is there. Very subtle, but there. A taste too, if you must know and children must know. I had to dip my finger deep inside the lily's mouth. It was damp, still moist from the overnight. When I slowly withdrew my small finger, I brought along a nearly translucent string, like spider's silk, attached to my finger. I tasted the lily dew, and it was sweet. Not too sweet like honey or a heavily perfumed rose petal, but just a hint of flowery water from the soft, milky bloom.

The pistil was another story. Initially, I didn't particularly like the pistils. Maybe it wasn't so much not liking as it seemed a little too stiff, too cocksure of itself (as most pistil and stamen are). For a time, I would cut them off to see if I liked the look of the calla lily without its bright-yellow protuberance. But, in the long haul, the pistil won out, as it seemed to balance the enormity of the flower, a single petal, larger than my two, tiny hands cupped as one.

Probing also led to a wondrous discovery about the lily. It was alive. As a child, these things are of great importance, especially when realized for the first time. If I held up the lily to the sun, and the light was just right, behind the seemingly thick skin of the petal were veins, the life force of this beautiful flower. Like the thin, blue lines running across my fair-skinned hands, there, hidden inside the lily were veins, threads of life like my own. Parents, teachers, and books all corroborated this profound discovery. And, when a child makes that leap to understanding the meaning of "all living things," it changes everything. It changes your life. It did mine.

The calla lily came home again just recently. Much has transpired over the last 40 years from those early days in Los

Gatos, California, where the lilies grew outside my bedroom window. I have moved and changed dramatically over those years, both physically and emotionally. But the sense of home came back to me when I witnessed those lilies again, this time in the Cape Winelands of South Africa, growing wild and in abundance.

In the many trips I've made to Africa, I have always felt a sense of home. Even before my first visit there, I was drawn to the continent. A sense of home, of place, cannot always be explained in words. We just know. More than anything, it is a feeling, a sense of familiarity and comfort, a place that speaks to us through our hearts. It does not always make sense. But you know it when you feel it, and there is no fighting, as you will surely lose. A sense of home has more to do than with where one was born. Our homes and foundations are discovered and created from a place that cannot always be found on a map. They are borne from the heart. It is not always the place that is the easiest. Far from it.

The lilies reminded me of that.

Driving through the lush winelands between the bucolic villages of Franschhoek and Stellenbosch, I was shocked to see open fields choked with calla lilies. These seas of creamy white were nestled beneath a blinding, blue sky and towering mountain ranges, jagged gnarls of stone, all heathered purple and dusky mauve. Pockets of the fertile land that were not covered with vines were lush with lilies. Thousands of them. All that life, the force of thousands of living calla lilies, brought home by an African sun that is brighter and more intense than I had ever seen. I imagined all those veins at work, nourishing these incredible flowers, masses of lily heads and proud pistils, paying homage to the sun. I yelled out to the person I was traveling with, "Look at all the calla lilies. They're everywhere!" Not so much looking for a response but rather for my own acknowledgment of familiar faces, flowers from my youth, where I was born. I was home.

Along the streets and dirt roads between villages, small children stood with outstretched arms. They were holding bundles of calla lilies for sale. The thick bundles, long stemmed, were more than half the size of the tiny bodies sometimes hidden behind the white heads. Tiny children with gigantic, prehistoric blooms clutched to their chests. Dark, beautiful faces, peeking out behind mammoth, white petals. Buckets filled with calla lilies lined the dirt roads. Lilies for sale. I never saw anyone stop and buy them. I didn't. I wish I had. I wondered what those children did every evening at dusk with all those lilies left behind. Did they probe? Did they cut off the sunny-yellow pistils to see what the flower looked like without its center? Did they taste the sweet flower water deep inside?

Back at my house in Maine, in the dead of winter, again I see white. But it is not the hopeful, creamy white of calla lilies. It is a landscape buried in deep snow. It's not the brilliant-blue sky of Africa, the blinding sun of the winelands before me, but the deep, steely gray of the sea, bordered by white snow and leaden skies. How I long for the lilies, for a place to call home. Adrift, I am at one of those places in life that offers no solid footing, no foundation. One of those places in between that we all must visit at one point or another. A place in between sun and shade, moonlight and darkness. In between meaning and uncertainty. It is the place of blurred focus in harsh reality that offers little light. But, alone in this darkness, I turn toward the sun, if only in my mind. I am moving toward a faraway sun, miles and miles away. And I see those cocksure, yellow pistils reaching skyward.

I see beautiful, brown faces, smiling behind cups of white blossom. It is not the easiest path. But the ocean in between will be crossed. And, when I step out, soaked and exhausted from the journey, I hope to feel solidity beneath my feet.

PART IV

The Places in Between

The world breaks everyone, and afterward, some are strong at the broken places.

~ Ernest Hemingway

CHAPTER 41

Today

It was my destiny to love and say goodbye.

~ Pablo Neruda

Here and now.

The last year has brought more heartbreak and loss. I am getting tired but determined to keep pressing on. Limping, for sure, but nonetheless moving. That is something, and, these days, I am grateful for small things.

I'm not sure if it is a function of aging or the barrage of life-changing experiences that have left me more concerned and determined to find my place in the world—how I fit in, and, of greater importance, how I can make a difference. Perhaps it is both. Maybe it's neither. Maybe it is simply being human. But it's a daily force within me, stronger than ever before, and I am struggling to find my way—and to have my voice heard in order to make that difference—no matter how big or small.

When we are young, we are constantly searching, much of the time unaware of what we are actually looking for, or hoping to find. But, nonetheless, the search matters—whether we "find" it or not—the searching, the delving into sometimes dark, foreign, or misunderstood places is half the getting there. Then, at some point, we drift into periods of complacency without even knowing it or when it settled in, overwhelmed with or just absorbed by life and all its complexities. As the years slip away, again we sometimes find ourselves in the elusive search for meaning, and, once more, the struggle itself is crucial and life affirming. It is when we allow ourselves to open up during the searching process, allowing for vulnerability and challenge, exposing ourselves completely, which, in turn, unfolds the thick, protective layers we've built up over time. The gift of time and our presumed longevity is not seen as inevitable any longer, and our sense of mortality and the unpredictability of life rides alongside us — not necessarily a burden, just a reminder, that's all. A reminder that each day counts; that each day can make a difference.

In witnessing firsthand, and being a part of so many of my loved ones' life and death struggles, it has opened my eyes to conditions I could have never imagined or known from a distance. It is often a terribly painful process, and we are wounded, no doubt. But I do believe it opens our eyes to the human experience and the struggles of all human beings, all living things. Compassion is perhaps the greatest emotion and depth of understanding, and meaning, that we can ever hope to experience. It brings down those self-erected walls we have built around ourselves — the fortresses of family and friends, of home and community, of all things familiar and safe — and leaves us naked and exposed in front of the world, the entire universe. It allows us to truly feel, perhaps for the first time, a collective heartbeat, and to see with one universal eye the suffering and plight of every life form on this planet. It is this connection with life that oftentimes eludes us. But, when we open ourselves to it, feel it, take it on, cradle and nurture it, the search for meaning in life begins to unfold in a singularly beautiful way, much like Emily Dickinson's line, "a ribbon at a time."

Lately, I have wondered if, in part, my connection, my spiritual sense of home with Africa has come from both conscious and unconscious sources, which has enabled me to better understand or relate to certain aspects of Africa, perhaps offering me a greater compassion for the peoples I met there. Maybe in an obscure way, growing up in a meager household, and experiencing early on how short and precarious life could be, contributed to my "pull" to the continent. I don't know, and, in truth, I suppose it doesn't really matter. The only thing of importance is the feeling deep within my gut, and my heart.

Africa is a continent where some life expectancies only reach into the 30s and 40s, maybe 50s at best. It is a place where people struggle for jobs and food and creature comforts that so much of the world takes for granted; where people struggle for education, for dignity, for good health, and for purpose—just like the rest of us. They seem to have a harder time attaining these things, not for lack of trying or ambition, certainly, but rather because of the myriad complexities that often plague the area.

Have my experiences and losses helped me to better understand these difficulties? Maybe, but only in the most minute of ways. Not for an instant do I claim to want for anything now (other than meaning and useful purpose) or while growing up, for that matter. Yes, at times we struggled financially. As very young children, we had gifts and bags of groceries delivered to our home by charitable organizations during the holiday season. We were on the "list" of those in need, those needing a helping hand in some way. Hand-me-downs, second-hand clothing, and belongings were what we knew, and that was fine. Children don't always know or feel poor unless living in poverty, which we were not. We had enough to eat and a roof over our heads, and the temperate, California climate allowed for being outdoors much of the time, playing, relatively healthy and happy. In a country where so many have so much, growing up without at times — particularly in an affluent area, which was my case — was not the norm. But, for me, it didn't have a negative or emotional residual effect, a stigma that clung tightly or obstructed hopes and dreams. If anything, early on, it made me realize my need to fulfill my dreams, to have a different life, a good life, and to make a difference.

John and I shared many visions, the most important being our outlook on life, the planet, the interconnectedness of all peoples and living things. Maybe the growing up in what would be labeled as "dysfunctional families" contributed in some way. I did not really know my father until nearly age three when he came to live under our roof, and for the first time. At age three, John had just lost his father. With the combined oddities and irregularities, the losses, we became survivors and individuals who were always taking care. We often found ourselves in the role of caregiver, and perennial bleeding hearts, for which I am grateful. I've always been amused at how the definition of "bleeding heart" is characterized by some as a personality flaw. I guess I will forever be amazed at how anyone can see caring or compassion as negative or shortsighted.

So, today, I am searching. I see more and more injustices in this world and cannot fathom how so many suffer and go unattended. When crises around the world, grand-scale suffering and destruction, are made public, if made public, by media who cringe at covering stories of real importance or substance, it is shamefully dilatory and hurried by meaningless sound bites. Sometimes, we need to be smacked over the head in order to get our full attention, which has been numbed and dumbed by so much inconsequential entertainment news. The world is bigger than we are. The stories are bigger than our personal tales. Perhaps we need to take a harder, closer look at universal loss and suffering, and how we fit in.

That said, and although our stories, our personal losses, are slight and maybe insignificant in light of the bigger picture, at the end of the day, the small tragedies unfolding beneath our roofs are what we are left with come early-morning light—the remains of our day.

Not long ago, my younger brother's near fatal car accident— a body shattered and broken, and ultimately filled with metal plates, pins, and screws—opened my eyes wider still. And, at the same time, a long-distance relationship that I had embraced and trusted later revealed a relationship of deceit; the person I had been involved with, a professor at a prestigious East Coast university, had turned out to be false; nearly all I had been told, and believed, were lies. We lived in different states, and I came to learn that lies are easily hidden at a distance. From a marriage borne of abiding love and trust, for the first time in my life I had entered into a relationship that was deceptive and evil, stripping me of any sense of trust in another human being, and no longer able to fully trust my heart, my instincts.

On the heels of it all, with no time to fully rebound, to find my equilibrium and to catch my breath, the losses continued to pile up. It began to feel like a horrible chain-reaction car wreck, one after the other—the carnage being some of those I loved most in life: two sisters-in-law; a best friend and soulmate in San Francisco, who, after a horrendous struggle coming to terms with a debilitating stroke, HIV, and substance abuse, took his own life; another best friend, who succumbed to cancer. No one lived out their fifth decade, and, yet again, still in my 40s, leaving me behind in the aftermath, in the twisted metal and carnage of once happy, young lives. Now gone, forever.

If not for the care and concern of two of my closest friends nearby, I am not sure I would have made it. And, at the same time, other good friends who knew what was unfolding and were initially of great support began to slip away, not able to cope with or unwilling to see my growing detachment and looming despondency. Many used to refer to me as "the rock," and maybe, seeing the rock crumbling, and for the first time, it was something they could not or did not want to face. Perhaps it was all too much—they had already dealt with a friend who had lost a husband. Maybe this was bordering on absurdity. But, with 3,000 miles between us, I couldn't have expected much, and there wasn't much they could be expected to do. And any small gesture over those long, silent months of darkness—a phone call, an email—would have shone a torch into the otherwise blackened abyss.

Without question, it was the darkest time of my life. And, if I thought that I had stepped into the final abyss while dealing with John's terminal illness and death, I was mistaken. It was the first time in my life that I questioned all that I knew, questioned life and existence, and if it was all worth it. I wondered why and how this could have happened to me—to so many of those I had loved so deeply. Why had I been left behind?

Little by little, that small ray of light shown again. I no longer knew where the path would lead, but I knew I had to take it. To one day love again, to trust again, and to hope again—no matter how painful. I had survived it all, and there was no way that now, although broken, I would not keep fighting.

As human beings, we are all, to a matter of degrees, walking wounded—raw, vulnerable, cautious, fearful. And yet, inevitably, most of us are still open to living and loving and hoping, all over again. Barely upright but moving, dragging ourselves, forward still. It is at times laughable, pathetic, and ultimately amazing. Not so unlike the reptile that loses an appendage and grows another one. Just like that.

So, like that animal, my life keeps going, growing, reinventing itself at times. And my heart continues to rebuild with so many pins and threads, staples and duct tape. It is barely holding together, but holding. I am planning. If for nothing more than today.

CHAPTER 42

Tomorrow

We know nothing of tomorrow;
our business is to be good and happy today.

~ Sydney Smith

The osprey are gone. The bats are out early. Hummingbirds too have begun their long, southward migration. Do they ride on the backs of the osprey, I wonder? The days are shorter now. And the nights seem longer than they used to be. The sun hangs heavy and red on the horizon, reluctant to fade away, dissolve into oblivion. But, unlike most of life, it is guaranteed another day. The moon, not far behind, anxiously awaits the sun's departure, eager to rise, to breathe its illumination across the encroaching darkness. Small light.

From all that I have learned, I have come to realize that I know very little. For all of the tomorrows I have lived, I will never know what the next one will bring, or take away. When we get too comfortable in the knowing, the perceived insight, inevitably, we are bluntly reminded of the unpredictability of it all—this life. Just when we think we've figured it out, the moon cracks. The sun weeps. Surety breeds the unexpected. Perhaps the best thing is not to get too comfortable with routine and complacency, with all that is familiar. Nothing remains the same, at least not for long.

I think of the losses I have endured over the last few years and, at times, cannot believe how many of those I deeply loved have departed from my life, forever. It is not easy being left behind. Another family member, suddenly gone. I had spoken with him a couple of weeks ago, his voice clear and strong. He seemed to be moving forward with his life, having lost so much, so much more than I have ever known. But he was quick to hide things, conceal his grief. Women cry, and men often bleed, silently. In the last two years, he had lost his beloved brother, sister, and wife—his entire family. But, finally, I thought I detected hope in his voice. Was it real or imagined? What he wanted me to hear, or what I needed to hear? We were, regardless of our footing, of comfort to each other now. Just the other day, I thought, "I'll call him tomorrow." John's younger brother, the last surviving sibling, gone. In his sleep, a heart attack, quick and painless. He was the same age as John when he died, just 52, and the last of the family name. No children—as close to tomorrow as we can ever hope to get. Sweet dreams, Clay. Tomorrow is more uncertain than we realize.

Time, the intangible, and healer of all wounds.

Recently too I received the sad news of a young man's death from ALS. And it reminded me of that day, over four years ago now, when John succumbed to the disease, and in return, the news unleashed that proverbial flood of emotion. Not that I needed reminding: Memories and emotions are always close to the surface. But, with time, they compartmentalize themselves somewhat, delicately closing inward, like a night blossom, knowing they will unfold again, a petal at a time, and when the time is right.

Terminal illness covers the gamut of emotions and response, in its poignancy and depth of human experience it makes us take a hard look at life and living, and what truly matters. Time, that elusive and intangible enigma, metamorphoses into a richness of moment. Suddenly, the length of life is not what constitutes living, but rather the detail and scope of each day become priceless. It is an amazing process. And the enveloping lightness—when the superficialities of the mundane are shed like a translucent skin, molted away, one by one, like so many feathers—is an unexpected gift in the otherwise fragmentary heaviness of fate.

> *Lives of great men all remind us*
> *We can make our lives sublime.*
> *And, departing, leave behind us*
> *Footprints on the sands of time.*

~ Longfellow

So, another season has come and gone. Another life cycle begins. And I know of only one other thing for sure that it will bring. As sure as the sun and the moon, it will bring change. It will deliver the unexpected, no matter how much we plan. Tomorrow is not entirely up to us. And, yet, I remain hopeful. How is that? Does that resilient little muscle, the heart, retain yet another perennial infinitesimal spot for hope?

The small light of the moon, on occasion, gives us glimpses of things we hope to come. Shimmering across the desert surface, perhaps not a beacon, but even the slimmest ray of light illuminates a path.

Afterword

A s usual, life took a few unexpected turns.
    Our beautiful home in Maine had become too large for me; there was overwhelming maintenance and cost, and, truth be told, without John, it no longer felt like home. I knew in my heart it was time to move on, and I put the house on the market. The weather too became more of a challenge than a blessing, and I began to spend winters in Mexico. I had never been to Mexico nor did I speak Spanish. But, following one particularly unbearable Maine winter, I had had enough. After watching a documentary on San Miguel de Allende and its vibrant literature and arts scene, and even though I had never heard of the town, I flew the coup. It was cheaper to rent there than to heat the house in Maine, I could work from anywhere as long as my laptop was in tow, and the culture offered something new and hopeful. And I wouldn't have to shovel my way out the front door.

    During the next couple of years, the U.S. economy began to falter, then crash. Between the deflated housing market and the stock market/financial crisis of 2007, both had devastating effects on millions of Americans, including me. The housing crisis hit rural Maine, and hard, long before it fully engulfed most of the United States, and homes began to sit — long term. A year passed without a single showing of my home, then another. I lost part of our life savings and retirement investments, my nest egg, in the market crisis. Coupled with the plummeting listing price of our home, my life took a turn I hadn't anticipated. My losses were nowhere near as great as so many, but my life options became decisively limited or, at the most hopeful, changed.

As the years slipped away, the once beautiful Victorian on the hill, overlooking the reach and saltwater cove, began to fall into disrepair. Without any promise of a sale, I made the decision to pack up a few boxes, send them down to Mexico, and rent for half the year at a time. Gradually, that turned into a year. Then, as another year passed without a sale, I stayed even longer in Mexico. I had left the house in Maine filled with everything I owned: cherished belongings, our library of hundreds of treasured books, family heirlooms, clothes, art, a kitchen fully stocked. I literally walked out and away—and locked the door behind me. It was not an easy decision to all but abandon my home, but I knew, for my own well-being, it was the only option.

Year in and year out, as the Maine house sat unlived in for much of the year, it was never broken into, nothing was ever taken. But, finally, after more than a handful of years going back and forth and leaving everything unattended, I went back to remove some of the few pieces that meant a great deal to me. I had been pushing my luck in keeping everything I owned in a vacant, old house by the sea, weather and fire—leaks from snow-heavy roofs, fallen trees, to a home built in 1885 of balloon framing overrun by mice, and wooden shingles—it was a potential disaster waiting to happen. I knew I had to set a few things aside. They were "soul anchors," as I called them, belongings that were of no real value other than to my heart and memory, the most valuable kind, which could never be replaced. I put those few belongings in a nearby storage unit.

On the eighth year, house unsold, still back and forth between Maine and multiple rentals in San Miguel de Allende, I thought I had a sale. I gave up the current rental in San Miguel, shipped my few boxes from Mexico back to Maine, but the sale never materialized. I had become an unintentional vagabond: moving back and forth, from one rental to the next, no real belongings with me, sleeping in the rentals of strangers, their beds, their belongings, with no solid footing or sense of home. For six years, this nomadic life had become my own. At this juncture, once again, and to be closer to family out west, I packed up a few things in Maine, had them shipped to my birthplace of Los Gatos, California, and rented a tiny apartment, sight unseen, and lived there for the next two years.

After nine years on the market, the Maine house finally sold. It was a huge financial and personal loss, barely selling for what I had bought it for some 20 years earlier, and before we had put a substantial amount of money into updates and renovations. What I was left with made clear that, financially, it was no longer an option to move back to California where I had family and old friends, and the only place that would have made sense to return. But, finally, I was able to cut loose the albatross, no matter how heartbreaking, and to say goodbye to what once was my home with John, to our friends, and to the bounty of wildlife that had thrived around our property. It was time to let go.

I flew back to Maine from California, to a 3,000-square-foot house filled with my life, once. I had six weeks to clear it out, 20 years of living, to sell most, give away what I could, and take with me perhaps 1% of my life, of my past. Going through those possessions and all of the memories—of my life with John, our families, photos—and deciding what would be gotten rid of, was one of the hardest times of my life. In some ways, having so little time to go through 20 years of memories allowed for a quick and judicious ridding of things, no matter how precious to me—and, in hindsight, some things should not have been sold, given, or thrown away, mostly my beloved books—but I had to make a decision, then and there. There was no real time for sentiment or second guessing.

Those few things that were the most precious in my life were put in boxes and taken to the nearby storage unit, eventually to be picked up by my brother and for his family, or things I loved and didn't trust to shipping that one day he would deliver to me. I got through the packing up and dissolving of not only 20 years of my life, but the belongings and memories of long passed family members. Those too, for the most part, were released.

At the end of six weeks, the house stood empty. I remember thinking how stunningly beautiful it looked with nothing in it—how the honey-toned wood floors and original Victorian woodwork and moldings shone in the warm, early-morning sunlight; how the windows, unadorned, opened onto the vast landscape of grass and crabapple trees, the stands of pines, the field of lupine, giving way to the saltwater cove, and to the sea. It had never looked more beautiful. I did it. And I had survived.

The generations of the crow family, which I had known and nurtured and loved for 20 years, remained. One particular crow, however, recognized me, even with all the time I had been coming and going, at times away for a year or more. Each day of my six weeks, I'd call for the morning feeding, and the crow family would swoop in from the cove and eat the scattered seed, the corn. One crow in particular would always stay. Then, early eve, just at dusk, when all birds should have been flying to their homes, their roosts, and settling in safe for the night, this one crow would stay behind for just a bit longer.

From my windows, I could watch it watching me. It perched on the deck post and watched me move from room to room, even as the last of the light faded from the sky. It knew. And I knew.

Leaving behind the wild and walking away from the animals I had come to nurture over the years—from the injured fox to myriad songbirds, chipmunks and squirrels, raccoons and skunks and porcupines—was one of the hardest things of all. They were, after all, family, especially the crows.

I left Maine exactly one day before the 10th anniversary of John's death. I returned to my small rental apartment in California and began my second international move: packing up, one last time, for a foreign place that would become my new home. However, back in Maine, the boxes I decided to ship had needed address labels, a destination, that of my new home. Knowing that my options were now limited, and exhausted from handling such a major life move, I knew the only place I could afford to live comfortably, and was close enough to California, was San Miguel de Allende. I knew the town and had made good friends. Housing was far less expensive, property taxes were next to nothing, and there was no need for a car. I could live well on very little, and want for even less. So the decision was made. The boxes that contained most of the remains of my life were sent to a larger storage facility in Bangor, Maine, to be shipped down at a later time. Then, barely having caught my breath, I flew back to California and began the process all over again.

In September 2012, two years after moving back to California, and after packing up both the Maine house and my apartment in Los Gatos, I flew southward—like a migrating bird—to my new home in Mexico. The few belongings I trusted to have shipped arrived. All but one box, which somehow got misplaced and, more than likely, was put in my small storage unit near my home in Maine, where the most precious, irreplaceable belongings were stored for my brother, and for delivery to me, one day down the road. In that particular box was my cherished recipe book, overflowing with family recipes, including the only copies of my grandmother's handwritten recipes.

A couple of months later, still settling into my new home in Mexico, I received an email from the owner of the storage facility near my old home in Maine. I was told that a flammable substance left in the warehouse by someone who had rented space for their vintage cars, and where 120 individual storage units were located, including mine, caught fire—an explosion and firestorm so massive that approximately 50 firefighters from neighboring towns were called in to fight the enormous blaze. Everything was reduced to ash. All 120 units filled with treasures, history, and family soul anchors, gone.

In my small unit were dozens of original and enlarged, 16x20, bromoil photographs by my late grandfather, some going back to the early 1930s. He had been written up in the Photographic Society of America journal as being one of the last practicing photographers of the bromoil technique in the United States. Along with those, his original oil paintings;

original stained glass windows my late father had designed; my grandmother's china; small, wooden figurines and keepsakes from the Black Forest region that my grandparents had brought with them in 1929 when they sailed into Ellis Island. Books and photographs, wedding gifts John and I had received, and so much more were now nothing more than dust. I had released much of what I had once "owned," taking only a small portion of those things that I wanted to hold close. What I had left behind were those additional invaluable objects that brought back the flood of memories when looked upon and touched, all memories that would fade somewhat without the richness of the tactile experience—the feel of my grandmother's old, wooden spoon in my hand, the one she had used every time to stir the dough for a hundred apple strudels.

I have learned along the way that nothing lasts forever. I've lost many of those I loved most in life; walked away from much of what I knew, what I had owned, and all that was once familiar. I know now that most things in life I can survive.

While my great love for John has never waned, I've also learned that time does heal, and many things do become easier as the years pass by. But I've also come to understand that some things get harder with the passage of time. The older I get, I find the longing for the simple things to be the hardest: the seemingly mundane day to day; the simple act of sharing anything, however small, with someone you love. I miss the breathing of John beside me, the sharing of a meal, a sunset, a laugh. I miss the companionship. I miss my travel partner. There is no doubt that most everything in this life is all the sweeter when shared.

Mexico had not been part of the plan. But it became my home, and I am fortunate. The years that have followed have opened new doors, particularly in travel. Suffering from an insatiable wanderlust since very young, living in Mexico has afforded me the continued opportunity to travel and experience new cultures. Home exchanging has become my savior — a wonderful and inexpensive way to travel long term and to live in beautiful parts of the world on very little. Exchanging homes has given me the gift of living for months at a time in big cities and small country villages; in homes with fully stocked kitchens where I can exercise my passion for cooking, shop the local markets, settle in, and feel a sense of belonging. Even better still, most of the exchange partners have now become good friends.

And, always, there will be Africa. I know with all of my heart that one day I shall return, and it will feel as though I've come home. I have been a lucky woman.

As I sit and write this from the desk in my sala, I look onto my inner courtyard patio. It is lovely. The vines have gotten wild over the last few years and spill across the stone face of the fountain, wonderfully unruly. I like them that way. The bougainvillea is an impossible shade of hot pink. The bamboo and palms have new, tender shoots. The summer iris, somehow, is blooming again, even though it's winter. I found an old hummingbird's nest in the tangle of vines not so long ago. All of 1 inch across, perfectly intact, a downy feather lining the small cup inside.

And so it goes.

San Miguel de Allende, Mexico
December, 2016

318

Resources

ALS Therapy Foundation: als.net
Project ALS: projectals.org
Gallmann Memorial Foundation: gallmannkenya.org
Jane Goodall Institute: janegoodall.org
Save the Elephants: savetheelephants.org
Big Life Foundation: biglife.org

One evening, during my stay at Kuki Gallmann's wildlife reserve in Kenya in 2003, she decided to invite a few friends to fly up to Ol ari Nyiro from Nairobi, to have dinner and stay the night. On the deck of Makena's Hills tented camp that evening, there were 10 of us around the table. Most of her guests were working for the United Nations, one working in the field in the Sudan, and all from various countries around the globe. There was one man, however, a British photographer, who was there to finish taking photographs of the African wild for a book. The next day, my late-afternoon bush drive with Douglas was cut short. While in the bush, we stopped to look at a rose-colored dusk, settling across Lake Baringo. Kuki radioed Douglas and said that the guest needed a few final shots before returning to Nairobi. Douglas would need to return to camp ASAP to take the photographer into the bush before nightfall. At first, I felt a little shortchanged. I could spend hours in the wild, and it would never be long enough. But I understood.

Years later, I came to know that the photographer at Ol ari Nyiro that night, who had needed just a few more shots of the wild for his book, was the wildlife photographer Nick Brandt. He had been working on his first book called *On This Earth*, a breathtaking photographic journey of some of the most beautiful, iconic, and endangered species in East Africa. It was to be the first of his trilogy on the decline of great African wildlife. In September 2010, in urgent response to the escalation of poaching in Africa due to increased demand from the Far East, Nick Brandt founded the nonprofit organization called Big Life Foundation, dedicated to the conservation of Africa's wildlife and ecosystems.

Made in the USA
Middletown, DE
24 May 2017